THIS DAY IN
FOOTBALL

THIS DAY IN
FOOTBALL

A DAY-BY-DAY RECORD OF THE
EVENTS THAT SHAPED THE GAME

T. J. TROUP

TAYLOR TRADE PUBLISHING
Lanham • New York • Boulder • Toronto • Plymouth, UK

Published by Taylor Trade Publishing
An imprint of The Rowman & Littlefield Publishing Group, Inc.
4501 Forbes Boulevard, Suite 200, Lanham, Maryland 20706
http://www.rlpgtrade.com

Estover Road, Plymouth PL6 7PY, United Kingdom

Distributed by National Book Network

British Library Cataloguing in Publication Information Available

Library of Congress Cataloging-in-Publication Data

Troup, T. J. (Terence Jon)
   This day in football : a day-by-day record of the events that shaped the game /
T. J. Troup.
       p.   cm.
   Includes bibliographical references.
   ISBN 978-1-58979-450-4 (pbk. : alk. paper)—ISBN 978-1-58979-452-8 (electronic)
   1. Football—History—Chronology.   I. Title.
GV950.T76   2009
796.332—dc22   2009018511

Printed in the United States of America

To Mary Jo Ann

Contents

Acknowledgments ix

Foreword xi

Introduction xiii

September 1

October 41

November 85

December 125

January 169

Acknowledgments

I would like to acknowledge the support of my family in the writing this book. Contributions also came from multiple sources: Jeff Anderson of the Vikings, Ryan Anderson of the Rams, Dan Edwards of the Jaguars, Pete Moris of the Chiefs, Craig Kelley of the Colts, Mike Eayrs of the Packers, Pete Fierle and Joe Horrigan at the Pro Football Hall of Fame, and Jennifer Allen Richards of the NFL Network.

Distinguished writers/historians Andy Piascik, Jim Campbell, and Abby Mendelson have given guidance when needed. John Richards's sense of humor was much appreciated at the times I needed it most.

Allen Barra and Paul Lionel Zimmerman have long provided insight and strong opinion on the men who played this game. In-depth research and data was gladly given by Eric Goska and Ken Pullis. Ira Gornick continues to amaze with his ability to clarify my thoughts on paper. Professor Suzanne Dolensky's historical perspective on garnering research has long been a source to help me wade through murky waters.

Acknowledgments

Finally, thanks to my friends at NFL Films, Kathy Davis, Chris Willis, and Ray Didinger, for all that they provided . . . and of course the "keeper of the flame" himself, Steve Sabol, for his steadfast inspiration.

Foreword

Football has been my life's work. I know the game mostly because I know its stories. And in the end, that's what history is, stories. But as a storyteller, I know personal narratives aren't always reliable. Time distorts. Memory plays tricks, which is why sometimes an old-timer recollecting his four-touchdown day in the mud and blood in 1942 turns out to be three touchdowns in three different games, all of them on sunny days, in 1944. Not that I mind. I love a good story, but sometimes getting the story right means getting the numbers right first.

But setting the record straight isn't easy, even for record-setting statistics. Take the mark for most touchdown receptions in a game. Lots of books can tell you that the Cardinals Bob Shaw snared five in one memorable game against the Colts, but only this book by T. J. Troup tells you what patterns he ran to do it. And it's the details that make the difference.

Not every record or statistic has a great story, of course, but they all have a context. Every play in every football game has a down and distance. Each snap occurs at a distinct place on the field and point in the season. And it's these variables that give statistics their meaning. So how does T. J. manage to put this dizzying array of numbers in perspective? Research. Lots and lots of research. Every year he comes to NFL Films and buries himself in our film vault for a week. The first couple of years he was here he was so immersed in the footage I barely saw him. I thought we'd have to go in with torches and rescue dogs to get him out. In fact, I think it's fair to say that, besides me, no one knows our film library better. Certainly no one loves it more, and it shows.

Hunkering down with dusty film canisters from the 1940s and pouring over play-by-play sheets isn't everyone's idea of a good time. It's painstaking, solitary work. It takes a genuine devotion to the game and, of course, a real head for numbers. T. J. has both and more. Turns out the man who I thought was collecting numbers was actually amassing stories; he just uses numbers instead of words to tell those stories. In his hands, figures come alive and stats dance across the page, each number a tiny part of a bigger picture. I'd call that a pretty neat trick if I didn't know better. But this book isn't a neat trick, it's a life's work. Open any page and you'll see it's been life well spent.

Steve Sabol
President, NFL Films

Introduction

So much has been achieved on the gridiron in the past 89 years by the men who have played this game of passion. Each of 153 days (September 1–January 31) is represented on the following pages.

Winning the game is a key component in the text, along with who did what if statistically significant to that game. To quote Paul Cezanne, "all art is selected detail," and though this book may not be artistic, the details are listed. As you, the reader, go through the pages, you might discover statistical discrepancies, which can all be explained. An example is the game between the Bears and the Rams on Sunday, September 26, 1965. The game was scheduled for the night before, but the riots in the Watts district of Los Angeles convinced the league and the Rams to move the game to Sunday, which I was present for.

In the 2nd quarter, Dick Butkus returns a Munson fumble (sack by Atkins) 11 yards to the Ram 18-yard line. On 1st down, Gale Sayers rolls left on a halfback option play, and when no receiver is open, he runs back to the right to score the 1st his record-setting 22 touchdowns in his rookie season. This is his only carry in the game. As to why George Halas refuses to play him on offense during the remainder of the game, we can only surmise. The rest of the Bear runners gained just 33 yards rushing on 18 attempts for the game. Though the Rams saw fit to correct the date on which the game was actually played, the Bears continue to list the game date as September 25 (and they also have an incorrect score).

Accomplishing one's goals is always rewarding, and if I am able to revive memories for fans of each of the teams, then a goal has been accomplished.

September

1

1991 The Eagles begin the season on the road against the Packers attempting to earn their fourth consecutive play-off berth. The outstanding Eagle defense dominates Green Bay in a 20–3 victory. Reggie White forces 2 fumbles, records 3 sacks, and deflects a Packer pass right to teammate Mike Golic (1 of 3 Eagle interceptions). Green Bay gains just 44 yards rushing, yet this is not surprising, since Philadelphia allows just 71 yards a game all season. The Eagle offense rallies behind Jim McMahon after a Bryce Paup hit on starting quarterback Randall Cunningham ends Cunningham's day. McMahon goes on to complete 17 of 25 for 257 yards, including a 75-yard bomb to Fred Barnett for a touchdown midway through the 4th quarter.

In their 10 wins during the season, the Eagle defense allows just 2 rushing touchdowns and 9 passing. Philadelphia leads the league in sacks with 55, records 48 takeaways, and allows only 184 yards total offense a game. Five Philadelphia defenders earn a Pro Bowl berth (Reggie White, Clyde Simmons, Jerome Brown, Seth Joyner, and Eric Allen). In their 6 losses, the Eagles score just 49 points;

thus they fall short of their destination in the NFL play-offs.

The Redskins have not earned back-to-back play-off berths since 1986 and 1987. Washington opens the season at home against a team they have dominated for more than 40 years, the Detroit Lions. Washington has won 12 consecutive games against the Lions and 20 of the last 23.

The Redskin defense allows Barry Sanders and his teammates just 154 yards of total offense. The Redskin attack gains 392, final score Washington 45, Detroit 0. The Lions recover from the loss and post their best season since 1962, while winning 12 games and a division title. They meet the Redskins again, in the NFC title game, with the same result, Redskins 41, Lions 10, as this legendary Redskin team goes on to win the Super Bowl.

2

1979 The New Orleans Saints have never had a winning season in their 12-year history, yet their best season was 1978 with a record of 7–9. They have had just one player chosen for the Pro Bowl in the entire decade (Archie Manning). Six times the Saints have beaten the Falcons, the most wins in team history against an opponent.

The Atlanta Falcons have had just two winning seasons in their 13-year team history but are coming off their first play-off season. Not one Falcon was chosen for the Pro Bowl for the 1978 season. The stage is set for one of the most exciting opening-day games in league history by two division rivals.

There are 70,940 fans in attendance at the Superdome, and the home crowd is not disappointed in the 1st half as

the Saints jump out to a 28–20 lead. Chuck Muncie sets a team record with 158 yards rushing, including a 69-yard scoring jaunt in the 2nd quarter. Muncie also throws a 40-yard touchdown pass to Wes Chandler in the 2nd quarter. Chandler is the first Saint in team history to catch passes for more than 200 yards in a game.

The 2nd half brings an Atlanta Falcon rally behind the punishing running of rookie William Andrews, who sets a team record with 167 yards rushing. Steve Bartkowski throws for 312 yards, and his main target is Alfred Jenkins, who catches 6 passes for 124 yards, yet it is Wally Francis with a 21-yard touchdown reception in the 4th quarter that finally puts the Falcons ahead, 34–31.

First-round draft pick Russell Erxleben, in his only game of the season, then kicks a 38-yard field goal to put the game into overtime. Need more drama? How about your rookie punter/place kicker attempting his first pass from his end zone in overtime in his first game? Erxleben's pass is intercepted by rookie reserve running back James Mayberry and returned 6 yards for the winning touchdown. The Saints achieve their first nonlosing season as they go 8–8, while Atlanta cannot sustain the play-off run and finishes 6–10.

1984 Five years to the date, and again we are in the Superdome. This time 66,652 fans witness not William Andrews but his backup, Gerald Riggs, doing the damage. Riggs breaks his teammate's record with 202 yards rushing on 35 attempts. The Falcons win the game, 36–28.

3

1995 The Rams, now relocated to St. Louis, are playing Green Bay on opening day. The Rams upset the play-off-

bound Packers, 17–14. Isaac Bruce scores the first touchdown on a 23-yard pass from Chris Miller in the 2nd quarter. Bruce catches 119 passes during the 1995 season to establish a new Ram record. During the season, Bruce has a six-game stretch were he catches 53 passes for 895 yards and 7 touchdowns. The Ram defense limits the Green Bay ground attack to 53 yards and intercepts Brett Favre 3 times.

2000   The Ravens are at Three Rivers Stadium to take on the Steelers. Running back Jerome Bettis of Pittsburgh gains just 8 yards on 9 carries, and the rest of the Steeler backs gain just 22 yards rushing, as the Ravens dominate the game in a 17–0 victory. The scoring punch for this opening-day victory is provided by wide receiver Qadry Ismail. He catches 7 passes for 102 yards and 2 touchdowns, including a 1st-quarter 53-yard strike from Tony Banks.

Opponents' not being able to run the ball effectively or score on the Raven defense is a consistent occurrence during the season. Baltimore sets new 16-game records as they allow only 970 yards rushing and 165 points. How consistent was this record-setting Raven defense? Baltimore allows only 8 offensive touchdowns in the 1st half all season and only 8 offensive touchdowns in the 2nd half all season. Although the stalwart Raven defense is chock full of strong defenders, 2 men stand-out: linebacker Ray Lewis and safety Rod Woodson. Earning a wild card berth during their first winning season in team history, the Ravens go on to win the Super Bowl in a dominating 34–7 victory over the Giants.

4

1983   Quarterback Lynn Dickey of the Packers returns to the Astrodome (he played four years for the Oilers) and

throws 5 touchdown passes as Green Bay prevails in overtime 41–38 against Houston. Dickey begins the game with 18 consecutive completions to set a new Packer record. Green Bay leads 28–10 at the half on 4 Dickey touchdown passes. Houston rallies in the 2nd half behind the passing of Archie Manning, who completes 22 of 34 for 348 yards, and Earl Campbell, who rushes for 123 yards on 27 carries and ties the score at 38.

The only Packer touchdown in the 2nd half is a 74-yard bomb to James Lofton (8 receptions for 154 yards) from Dickey. Dickey leaves the game due to illness after completing 27 of 31 for 333 yards. In overtime, it is David Whitehurst who leads Green Bay on a 59-yard drive culminating in future Hall of Fame kicker Jan Stenerud's 42-yard game-winning field goal. This opening-day loss by Houston keeps them in a downward spiral, as the Oilers go on to lose 39 of 45 games from November 15, 1981, through November 4, 1984.

1994 It is opening day in Indianapolis and rookie running back Marshall Faulk's debut as a Colt. Faulk gains 143 yards rushing on 23 carries and scores 3 touchdowns in the Colts' 45–21 victory over the Oilers. This future Hall of Famer will finish fifth in the league in rushing with 1,282 yards. The 45 points represent the most points scored on opening day in Colt history, breaking the record of 38 set by the John Unitas–led Colts of 1967. The Colt defense limits Houston to just 79 yards rushing and records 4 sacks and 3 takeaways, including Tony Bennett's 75-yard fumble return for a touchdown in the 2nd quarter.

5

1937 It is the first game of the 1937 season, and we are in Pittsburgh at Forbes Field for the battle between the

Philadelphia Eagles and the Pittsburgh Pirates. John Victor McNally has played 118 games in his already legendary career. He has set records for pass receiving and touchdowns on interception returns, yet this game is a first: his first as player/coach for Art Rooney's Pirates.

Philadelphia ties the game at 14 in the 4th quarter and then kicks off to Johnny "Blood," and the vagabond halfback returns the ball 92 yards for a touchdown. Tailback Max Fiske throws to McNally for 44 yards and a touchdown later in the quarter to seal the Pittsburgh victory. Johnny is the first Pittsburgh player to catch a touchdown pass and return a kickoff for a touchdown in the same game. The 27 points scored by Pittsburgh remain the season high, and the Pirates win just three more games in McNally's first season as coach.

1993 The Cleveland Browns open the season at home against the rival Bengals. Outside linebacker Clay Matthews establishes a new team record as he plays in his 217th game. Led by Matthews, the Browns defense shuts down the Cincinnati ground attack, as the Bengals gain just 55 yards on 20 rushing attempts. Cleveland overcomes an early 14-point lead and romps to a 27–14 victory.

Behind 3–2 in the 2nd quarter, Brett Favre hits Sterling Sharpe with a 50-yard touchdown pass to give the Packers a lead they never relinquish. Sharpe catches 7 passes for 120 yards (his 20th game of 100 yards or more receiving) as Green Bay defeats the Rams, 36–6. Sharpe goes on to lead the league with 112 receptions for the season and breaks his own team receiving record set the year before of 108.

6

1981 The Dallas Cowboys embark on their quest to earn a play-off berth for the seventh consecutive season. Dallas is on the road against longtime bitter rivals, the Redskins. Welcome to Washington, Joe Gibbs; for your first game as head coach you face the legendary Tom Landry. The Dallas offense is paced by future Hall of Famer Tony Dorsett, who rushes for 132 yards on 21 carries in the Cowboy 26–10 victory. The Cowboys dominate when Dorsett rushes for more than 100 yards, with a record at this point of his career of 18 wins and 1 loss. The Dallas "Doomsday" defense limits the Skins to just 44 yards rushing, while intercepting 4 Joe Theismann passes. One of the interceptions is by rookie Everson Walls, who goes on to lead the league with 11. The Cowboys again advance to the NFC Championship Game to face the Bill Walsh–led San Francisco 49ers.

The Bengals have won just 14 of their last 49 games and open the season at home against Seattle. For the first time in their 14 year history, the Bengals are down by 21 points in the 1st quarter. Turk Schonert enters the game in the 2nd quarter, and the rally begins. Cincinnati gains 210 yards rushing, while the Bengal defense records 3 sacks and 4 takeaways in a 27–21 victory. Rookie wide receiver Chris Collinsworth makes his debut with 4 catches for 65 yards and goes on to gain more than 1,000 yards receiving for the season. Cincinnati finishes 12–4 for the season and advances to the Super Bowl for the first time in team history.

1998 The Vikings begin their record-setting season at home with a 31–7 victory over the Buccaneers. Minnesota continues on to score 556 points for the season, an average of just under 35 points a game. Minnesota goes on to win 15 games and host the NFC Championship Game against the Atlanta Falcons.

7

1963   Former San Diego Charger assistant coach Al Davis is now the head coach of the Oakland Raiders, a team that has won just 2 of their last 24 games. A revised roster and new optimism is in place as the Raiders travel to Houston to take on the three-time Eastern Division champion Oilers at Jeppesen Stadium on a Saturday evening.

Houston leads 6–0 at the half on 2 George Blanda field goals. The aggressive Raiders commit 17 penalties in the game, but they also take the ball away from the Oilers 10 times. Free safety Tommy Morrow sets a Raider record as he intercepts 3 passes (he later sets a league record that still stands with interceptions in eight consecutive games), and he earns first team all-league honors.

Ahead 10–6 entering the 4th quarter, quarterback Tom Flores hits Art Powell (another of Coach Davis's roster additions) with an 85-yard touchdown pass. In his first game as a Raider, Powell catches 7 passes for a team record 181 yards. Oakland wins 24–13 and goes on to win an additional nine games for the greatest turnaround in pro football history at this point in time.

1981   Prolific passing was the trademark for both Brian Sipe of the Browns and Dan Fouts of the Chargers in 1980. They both threw for more than 4,000 yards and now rank among the top four for all-time completions in a season. They both threw 30 touchdown passes in the regular season and lost in the play-offs to the eventual Super Bowl champion Raiders.

It is the first Monday night game of the season, and we are in Cleveland as these two field generals square off. Although Sipe sets team records for completions in a game with 31 and attempts with 57, it is Fouts with 15 consecutive completions at one point in the game and 330 yards on his 19 completions that decides the match up. Future Hall of Fame wide receiver Charlie Joiner is Fouts's main target, as he catches 6 passes for 191 yards. Running back Chuck Muncie ably assists the Charger offense with 161 yards rushing as San Diego dominates 44–14. The Chargers again play in the AFC Championship Game and lose, yet again.

8

1985 Although the New England Patriots have won just 24 of their last 57 games, they are poised to contend. Leadership is being provided by Coach Raymond Berry and a strong core of veterans led by Pro Bowl offensive guard John Hannah and Pro Bowl inside linebacker Steve Nelson.

The Patriots open the season at home against the Green Bay Packers before 49,488 fans. Green Bay's running attack is stonewalled by the Patriot defense as they gain just 59 yards rushing on 19 attempts. The Patriots allow just 103 yards a game rushing all season. Future Hall of Fame left outside linebacker Andre Tippett records 3 of New England's 7 sacks to keep pressure on Lynn Dickey the entire game.

Quarterback Tony Eason of New England completes 21 passes for 241 yards. Holding a 19–6 4th quarter lead, running back Craig James breaks free on a 65-yard touchdown run. New England averages 145 yards a game on the ground. Green Bay scores twice late to bring the final score to 26–20.

2002   The Oakland Raiders have earned a play-off berth the past two seasons, but this proud organization has designs on another Super Bowl. The Raiders open the season at home against the Seattle Seahawks before 53,260 fans in the "Black Hole." Quarterback Rich Gannon spreads his 19 completions around to eight different receivers, but the key man in the Raider offense is running back Charlie Garner, who gains 191 yards rushing and receiving, while scoring 2 touchdowns in the 31–17 Oakland victory. The silver and black shut down the Seahawk running game as they gain only 43 yards on 16 attempts. This is a harbinger of things to come, as the Raider defense allows only 91 yards a game rushing all season.

   Rich Gannon sets a new record for most completions in a season with 418, as he gains 4,689 yards passing. The Raiders lead the league in total 1st downs with 366 and points scored with 450. The Raiders advance to the Super Bowl for the fifth time in their history.

9

1961   The defending league champion Oilers open their season at Jeppesen Stadium with a 55–0 demolition of the Raiders (still their largest margin of victory in team history). Charley Tolar records his first 100-yard rushing game (101 on 18 carries), and all-league receiver Charley Hennigan gains 113 receiving (including a 78-yard score in the 2nd quarter). Hennigan goes on to gain 1,746 yards receiving to establish a new record and post ten 100-yard receiving games in a season, also a new record. The Oiler defense limits the Raiders to 99 yards total offense and takes the ball away 5 times. The key man in this game is consensus all-pro left corner Tony Banfield, who intercepts twice (including 1 in the end zone to stop a Raider scoring threat).

1979 The Patriots open the season by setting records for points scored in a game (56), greatest margin of victory (53), and total yards gained in a game (597). Steve Grogan completes 13 of 18 passes for 315 yards and a record tying 5 touchdown passes. Harold Jackson catches 3 passes (all for touchdowns) for 121 yards. Stanley Morgan catches 3 passes for 102 yards and 2 touchdowns. Jet quarterbacks are sacked 9 times for 86 yards in the game, and the opportunistic Patriot defense also records 6 takeaways in the 56–3 victory.

1990 The Houston Oilers earned three consecutive playoff berths from 1987 to 1989 under the direction of Jerry Glanville. Glanville is now the head coach of the Atlanta Falcons, and we are in the Georgia Dome to open the season. The Falcons are quick out of the gate with a 21-point 1st quarter (still a team record). Included in the scoring are 2 fumble returns for a touchdown, the first by Bobby Butler in the end zone and the second a 65-yard trundle by linebacker Jessie Tuggle. This is the 2nd of his record-setting 5 fumble returns for a touchdown.

Quarterback Warren Moon of the Oilers completes 31 of 52 for 397 yards and 4 touchdowns, but it is not enough in the Atlanta 47–27 win. This Falcon victory is the highlight of the season, as they win only five games. Houston, on the other hand, rebounds from the opening day loss and again earns a wild card berth with a 9–7 season.

10

1967 Due to injury on the defensive line and excellent depth in their linebacker corps, the Oakland Raiders begin the season in a 3–4 defense. The Bronco air attack completes just 2 of 16 for 17 yards. Add to that the Raider pass rush that records 7 sacks for 70 yards. Denver finishes with −53 passing in the Raider 51–0 victory.

The two new quarterbacks that Al Davis has acquired pay immediate dividends, as both Daryle Lamonica and George Blanda throw touchdown passes. Blanda also kicks his first field goal as a Raider. Denver continues to struggle all season and finishes fourth in the AFL West, while Oakland becomes the first team in AFL history to win 13 regular-season games.

1989 From 1974 through 1985, the Steelers beat the Browns 18 of 24 times. It is the first meeting during the 1989 season between these two bitter rivals, and Cleveland has won six straight games from Pittsburgh. The Browns erupt for 44 points in the first 3 quarters. Dave Grayson becomes the first Brown to return both an interception and a fumble for a touchdown in the same game in Cleveland's 51–0 destruction of Pittsburgh.

Veteran all-pro linebacker Clay Matthews opens the scoring by also returning a fumble for a touchdown and helps guide new head coach Bud Carson's defense. The Steelers gain just 84 yards on 10 completions but lose 67 yards when sacked 6 times. The usual staunch Steeler ground attack gains only 36 yards, thus total offense of just 53 yards for the day.

Cleveland returns to the AFC Championship for the third time in four years, and Pittsburgh overcomes this rocky start and improves steadily during the season. Pittsburgh joins Cleveland in the play-offs as they earn a wild card berth.

2000 Jimmy Smith sets the Jaguar record with 291 receiving yards (the fifth highest in league history at that time) on 15 receptions and 3 touchdowns in a 39–36 loss to the Baltimore Ravens. Smith will earn his fourth consecutive Pro Bowl berth during the 2000 season. The Ravens allow only 129 points in their other 15 games during the regular season.

11

1938 The defending league champion Redskins open the season at Municipal Stadium in Philadelphia. Max Krause scores his only 3 touchdowns of the season in this game and records the only 100-yard rushing performance of his career (132 yards on just 6 carries). Krause puts the Skins ahead with a 48-yard run. Just before the half and now down 16–7, Sammy Baugh is smashed into the turf as he attempts to pass. Baugh completes this final pass for 57 yards and a touchdown to Krause (Baugh completed 12 of 13 for the game) just before the half. Krause gets the lead back for the Skins on a 71-yard run on a reverse in the 3rd quarter. The Eagles fight back and take the lead again. Rookie tailback Bill Hartman completes a pass on a tackle-eligible play out of a spread formation with an unbalanced line to Bill Young for 62 yards and the winning score in a 26–23 victory.

1965 The defending league champion Buffalo Bills open their season before 45,502 fans (largest crowd up to this time) at War Memorial Stadium against the Patriots. Led by "Big Ses" (Tom Sestak), the Bills defense continues their legendary defensive streak of not allowing an opponent to rush for a touchdown. For 16 games (October 24, 1964–October 31, 1965), Buffalo allows just 971 yards rushing on 349 attempts (2.8 a carry). Five key interceptions by the Bills also aid the cause in the 24–7 victory.

1966 It is one year later, and again the Bills are defending league champions. The Kansas City Chiefs defeat the Bills in War Memorial Stadium 42–20 for their first victory over Buffalo in four years. Chiefs rookie Mike Garrett returns a punt 79 yards for a touchdown in the 3rd quarter, and Ed Rutkowski of the Bills returns a punt 73 yards for a touchdown in the 4th quarter (the only time in AFL history both teams return a punt for a touchdown).

1983 The Cleveland Browns defeat the Lions 31–26 in Detroit as Brian Sipe becomes the all-time leader in touchdown passes thrown in team history with 135. Four-time Pro Bowl defensive tackle Doug English ties Ted Hendricks record for safeties in a career with 4 when he sacks Brian Sipe in the end zone in the 4th quarter.

12

1965 The Raiders open their last season at Frank Youell Field with a 37–10 rout of the Kansas City Chiefs. When Tom Flores is knocked out of the game in the 2nd quarter, Dick Wood replaces him and runs and throws for 3 touchdowns. The revamped Raider secondary, with corner Kent McCloughan and all-league Dave Grayson, allows Kansas City only 6 completions for 61 yards on 27 attempts.

Claude "Hoot" Gibson returns his 3rd punt for a touchdown as a Raider for the final score. Oakland goes on to finish the season with an 8–5–1 record in Al Davis's last season as head coach.

1976   Including the play-offs, the Raiders had lost five of their last seven games to the Steelers and trailed 28–14 with 6:43 left in the 4th quarter at home to open the season. The Raiders will not be denied today, as league passing efficiency champion Ken Stabler (103.4) gains 342 yards passing against a Steeler secondary that will lead the AFC with a defensive rating of 45.2. Future Hall of Fame tight end Dave Casper catches 7 passes for 124 yards to aid Stabler in the 31–28 victory (rookie Fred Steinfort kicks the winning field goal with 18 seconds left).

Pittsburgh, after a 1–4 start, rallies to win nine consecutive games behind a defense that allows only 28 total points and 183 yards a game total offense. The 13–1 Raiders gain more than 5,000 yards in total offense and meet their bitter black and gold rivals in the play-offs for a record fifth consecutive season.

1982   Former Raider assistant coach Bill Walsh and his defending Super Bowl champion 49ers host the Raiders for the season opener. Rookie Marcus Allen gains more than 100 yards rushing for the first of his team record 22 times and scores his first NFL touchdown in the Raiders 23–17 victory. The rugged Raider defense, led by future Hall of Famers Ted Hendricks and Howie Long, stonewalls the San Francisco running game (60 yards on 22 attempts). The Raiders go on to earn a play-off berth in the 16-team tournament, as Allen leads the league in scoring and touchdowns.

13

1964 The Vikings open the season with a surprising 34–24 victory over the Baltimore Colts at Metropolitan Stadium. Minnesota sets a team record that stands 43 years as the Vikes gain 313 yards rushing. For the only time in team history, Viking teammates gain more than 100 yards rushing as Pro Bowl–bound Tommy Mason gains 137 on 20 carries and Bill Brown gains 103 on 20 carries. The 463 yards of total offense gained by Minnesota is the most allowed by Baltimore all season. Minnesota goes on to post their first winning season in team history, while the Colts rebound to win the Western Conference with a record of 12–2.

1992 The 49ers are at home to take on the defending AFC champion Buffalo Bills and go on to set a team record by gaining 598 yards of total offense, yet they lose the game 34–31. Multiple records are set in this now legendary game. Jim Kelly is the first Bills quarterback to throw for more than 400 yards (22 of 33 for 403). For the third time in league history, opponent passers throw for more than 400 yards, as league passing efficiency champion Steve Young gains 447 passing on his 26 completions. Both teams have duos that gain more than 100 yards receiving, Buffalo with Andre Reed and Pete Metzelaars, San Francisco with John Taylor and Mike Sherrard.

The Bills overcome a 24–17 halftime deficit and drive 72 yards for the winning score in the 4th quarter on a Thurman Thomas 11-yard run. Mike Cofer misses a 47-yard game-tying field goal with 54 seconds left. The 1,086 total yards is the fourth most in league history, and amazingly for the first time in league history, neither team punts the ball.

1998   The defending Super Bowl champion Denver Broncos dominate the Dallas Cowboys 42–23 at Mile High Stadium. Terrell Davis gains 191 yards rushing and explodes on touchdown runs of 63 and 59 yards in the 1st quarter. Denver, with 35, scores more points in a half against Dallas than any opponent in Cowboy history. The outstanding Bronco receiving corps of Shannon Sharpe, Ed McCaffrey, and Rod Smith gain 290 yards on 15 receptions. Davis gains more than 2,000 yards rushing for a Denver team that scores more than 500 points and goes on to defend their Super Bowl title.

14

1969   Kansas City opens the season on the road in San Diego with a 27–9 victory. Future Hall of Famer Len Dawson throws two 2nd-half touchdown passes to Otis Taylor to ignite the offense. Although Dawson is injured part of the season, the Chiefs offensive line grinds away, as Kansas City leads the AFL in team rushing with 2,220 yards.

Defensively, the Chiefs set league records as they allow only 16 offensive touchdowns for the season. Kansas City opponents gain the fewest total yards in league history with just 3,163 (226 a game). Led by all-time AFL free safety Johnny Robinson, the Chiefs lead the league in pass defense efficiency with a mark of 42.1. Robinson has four future Hall of Famers on defense with him (Willie Lanier, Bobby Bell, Buck Buchanan, and Emmitt Thomas). The Chiefs go on to earn a play-off berth, defeat the last two AFL champions (the Jets and the Raiders), and have a date with destiny in New Orleans in January.

1980   The Raiders are in San Diego to battle their longtime rivals for AFC West supremacy. Due to Willie Jones's

11-yard fumble return, Oakland leads 17–10 at the end of the 3rd quarter. Jim Plunkett's touchdown pass to Raymond Chester ties the game in the 4th quarter. Future Hall of Famer Dan Fouts passes for 363 yards on 28 completions, yet he saves his best for last as he fires to John Jefferson for 24 yards and the winning score. Jefferson and Kellen Winslow combine for 18 catches and 242 yards.

Fouts continues on to break his own record for yards passing in a season with 4,715 and lead the Chargers to a second consecutive AFC West title. San Diego goes on to meet the Raiders in the AFC Championship Game in January.

2003   Jamal Lewis of the Ravens sets the record for most yards gained rushing in a game with 295 on 30 carries (including touchdown runs of 82 and 63 yards) in a 33–13 decision over the Browns. In the rematch later in the season, Lewis gains 205 yards on 22 carries to set another record. He is the only man in league history to rush for 500 yards against a division opponent in a season. Cleveland gains just 138 yards on 44 rushing attempts in the two games. The combination of strong run defense and a powerful running game earns Baltimore a wild card berth in the play-offs.

15

1940   The Lions are on the road, but instead of playing the Cardinals in Comiskey Park, we are in Buffalo. There is much more mud and rain than total offense in this game, as both teams combine to gain a total of 30 yards (still the record today). Marshall Goldberg of the Cardinals is the standout in this game, as he gains 26 yards rushing on 8 carries.

In the 3rd quarter, tailback Dwight Sloan of the Lions completes a pass to Lloyd "Wild Hoss" Cardwell for 27 yards and 1st and goal at the Cardinal 1-yard line. Goldberg, who makes the game-saving tackle, proceeds to knife into the Lion backfield to dump Sloan for a 5-yard loss. On 3rd down, Gaynell Tinsley intercepts Sloan to stop the threat. Even eight 1st down quick kicks in the 4th quarter by both teams cannot force a turnover, thus a 0–0 tie.

1968 The Raiders have won 20 of their last 24 games and open the season in Buffalo as defending league champions. The Bills are about to embark on the worst season in team history. Paul Maguire's 1st punt is returned by rookie left corner George Atkinson 86 yards for a touchdown. Maguire's next punt is returned by Atkinson 54 yards to the Buffalo 9-yard line. Atkinson later returns 3 more punts for 65 yards, setting a league record for punt return yardage in a game.

The Raider vertical air game is not up to par, yet Daryle Lamonica completes a 57-yard strike to Warren Wells late in the 1st quarter to put the Raiders ahead, 21–0. Oakland's brutally effective ground game is in high gear, however, as they pound out 210 yards on 35 attempts. Hewitt Dixon goes over the century mark for the first time, with 104 yards on just 16 carries.

Rookie Dan Darragh of the Bills completes just 4 of 20 pass attempts, and Kay Stephenson in his first action as a Bill does not complete a pass. The Oakland defensive line destroys the Buffalo pass pocket with 8 sacks for 94 yards; thus Buffalo loses 19 yards passing for the game. Buffalo gains 210 rushing, and this leads to their only touchdown early in the 4th quarter. The final score is Oakland 48, Buffalo 6. The Raiders return to the AFL title game against the Jets. Buffalo wins just one game all season (also against the Jets).

16

1938   It is a Friday night in Buffalo Civic Stadium, and the Eagles take a 27–7 victory over the Pittsburgh Pirates. Jay Arnold becomes the only Eagle in team history to score a touchdown on a fumble return, an interception, and a pass reception in a game (all in the 1st half). It is the first time in his career he has scored a touchdown, and goes on to record only 3 more touchdowns in his 50-game career.

1973   The debut of Chuck Knox as Rams coach begins in Kansas City with a 23–13 victory. For the fifth time in team history, the Rams have teammates rush for more than 100 yards each (Lawrence McCutcheon 120 on 21 carries and Jim Bertelsen 143 on 28 carries). Veteran John Hadl, in his first game as Ram quarterback, throws sparingly but effectively as he completes 8 of 10 for 99 yards and 2 touchdowns (including a 31-yard scoring toss to McCutcheon in the 2nd quarter).

The rugged Ram defense allows the Chiefs just 40 yards rushing on 21 carries. This is a harbinger of things to come, as Los Angeles allows just 79 yards a game rushing to lead the league. Future Hall of Famer Merlin Olsen earns his 12th Pro Bowl berth and future Hall of Famer Jack Youngblood his first. Knox's first season is an overwhelming success as the 12–2 Rams (the two losses are by a combined 3 points) return to the play-offs for the first time in four years.

1979 Future Hall of Famers Walter Payton and Tony Dorsett bring their 2–0 teams into Texas Stadium for this marquee match up. Both warriors gain more than 100 yards rushing, yet the difference in the game will come via the pass.

Rookie Vince Evans gains 155 yards on his 5 completions, with 2 touchdowns. He is outdone by "Captain Comeback" Roger Staubach in a game that has 6 lead changes. The winning score is a 22-yard touchdown pass from Staubach (18 of 31 for 222 yards) to Tony Hill in the 4th quarter in the Cowboys 24–20 win.

17

1961 Sam Etcheverry, in his very first NFL game for St. Louis, sets a new league record as he fumbles 6 times (he recovers 4) in a 21–10 victory over the Giants at Yankee Stadium. After a scoreless 1st quarter, Don Owens of the Cardinals strips the ball from Bobby Gaiters, and left corner Willie West recovers in the end zone.

New York regains the lead in the 2nd half, but Cardinal defensive coach Chuck Drulis utilizes safeties Jerry Norton and Larry Wilson on the blitz to keep St. Louis in the game. New York quarterbacks are sacked 5 times, gain only 157 yards in total offense, and turn the ball over 5 times, including Jerry Norton's 13-yard interception return into Giant territory late in the 4th quarter. Etcheverry completes a screen pass to fullback Frank Mestnik for 5 yards for the final touchdown.

The Cardinals, who expected to contend for the Eastern Conference championship, cannot maintain the momentum with this victory, and coach Pop Ivy resigns with a 5–7 record. New York rebounds from the loss and wins the East with a 10–3–1 record.

1978 The defending Super Bowl champion Dallas Cowboys have won 27 of their last 32 games. They are in the Coliseum to play the undefeated Rams (2–0). Three times in the last five seasons they have played each other in the play-offs, yet only twice in the regular season.

On 3rd and 18 on their 1st possession, future Hall of Fame quarterback Roger Staubach is intercepted by Billy Simpson (whose 28-yard return sets up John Cappelletti's 1-yard run). Future Hall of Fame running back Tony Dorsett has gained 258 yards on 39 carries in the first two games of the 1978 season, but today he gains just 38 on 19 carries. The Ram pass rush sacks Staubach 3 times and intercepts him 4 times, including Rod Perry's game-clinching 43-yard touchdown return in the 4th quarter. Wide receiver Ron Jessie stars on offense for the Rams with 7 catches for 144 yards. The Rams go on to win the NFC West and host Dallas (winners again of the NFC East) in the NFC title game in January.

18

1960 In their first-ever game at War Memorial Stadium, the Bills lead at halftime, 13–6. Two Frank Tripucka touchdown passes in the 3rd quarter put Denver ahead, 20–13. Tom O'Connell hits Elbert "Golden Wheels" Dubenion with his 2nd touchdown bomb of the game (Dubenion, with 112 yards, has the first 100-yard receiving game in Bills history). The Bills insert Bob Broadhead at quarterback, and he scores a 2-point conversion to give Buffalo the lead. An O'Connell pass in the 4th quarter is intercepted by right corner John Pyeatt, who sprints 40 yards for the winning score. The defensive hero for Denver, however, is Austin "Goose" Gonsoulin (wearing jersey number 45), who is the first player in AFL history to intercept 4 passes in a game. Gonsoulin goes on to lead the league in interceptions with 11 (still the team record).

1966 The Dallas Cowboys, in a quest of their first division title, are in the Cotton Bowl to host the New York Giants. Guns a blazin', the Cowboys offense fires up 45 points and 518 yards in total offense. Don Meredith ties Eddie Lebaron's team record with 5 touchdown passes. Both Dan Reeves (120) and Bob Hayes (195) gain more than 100 yards receiving, while catching all 5 touchdown passes. The Cowboy defense does its part, as left corner Cornell Green returns an errant Giant pass 41 yards for the final touchdown in a 52–7 victory.

1977 The Chicago Bears have won just 35 of their last 113 games, yet optimism reigns supreme as the Bears open the season at Soldier Field against the Detroit Lions. Walter Payton gains 160 yards rushing on his way to the league rushing title with 1,852 yards (just the fourth time a player has rushed for more than 1,800). His 73-yard run on a draw play (longest run at Soldier Field at this point in time) in the 1st quarter sets up the 1st touchdown for the Bears in the 30–20 Chicago victory. The Bear pass rush does its part with 6 sacks on Greg Landry. Chicago advances to the play-offs for the first time in 14 seasons.

19

1965 The defending Western Conference champion Colts open the season with a 35–16 victory over the Vikings at

Memorial Stadium. Future Hall of Famer Lenny Moore continues his record-setting pace as he runs for a touchdown for his 11th consecutive game. The Colts overcome an early 10-point deficit as John Unitas completes 12 of the last 13 passes for two 2nd-half touchdowns to Jimmy Orr and John Mackey. Pro Bowl safety Jerry Logan's 38-yard touchdown on an interception gives Baltimore the lead just before the half. The resilient Colts remain in the race for the Western Conference title all season.

1971 The defending AFC Central Division champion Bengals open the season at Riverfront Stadium against the Eagles. Quarterback Virgil Carter completes 22 of 33 for 273 yards and 3 touchdowns in the 37–14 victory. Carter hits Speedy Thomas with a 90-yard touchdown strike in the 3rd quarter (the longest completion in the league for the 1971 season), and Carter continues on to lead the league in completion percentage at 62.2.

Essex Johnson gains 113 yards rushing on just 8 carries (including a 68-yard dash in the 4th quarter) to give the Bill Walsh–led offense the balance he desires. Cincinnati's defense, led by Bill Bergey and Mike Reid, stonewalls the Eagles. They allow a team record of only 39 yards rushing (at this point in team history). Pro Bowl left corner Lemar Parrish records 1 of the 3 interceptions in this dominant performance.

1982 The Jets, hoping to rebound from an opening-day loss, are on the road to play their bitter rivals, the Patriots. In one of their most impressive performances in team history, the Jets win 31–7 (the first of five straight wins). The Patriots gain only 57 yards for the entire game (their fewest since November of 1970 against the Jets), including −4 passing. Matt Cavanaugh completes just 6 of 17 for 64 yards and is sacked 6 times for 68 yards.

League rushing champion Freeman McNeil gains 106 yards rushing on 19 carries (he goes on to lead the league with a 5.2 average per rush). McNeil keys an offense that records thirty 1st downs in the game (the most ever allowed by the Patriots at this point in team history). New York returns to the play-offs.

20

1970 The merger allows the best second-place team from each conference to earn a play-off berth, known as the "wild card." The Lions, who closed with a rush (6–1–1) to end the 1969 season, open in Green Bay and for the first time in 36 years shut out the Packers 40–0. Detroit gains their fifth most rushing yards in a game (at this point in team history) with 266. Mel Farr and Altie Taylor combine to gain 144 yards on 33 carries. Larcenous left corner Lem Barney, who has intercepted 18 passes in his last 29 games, returns an interception 40 yards for a touchdown in the 3rd quarter to seal the game. Detroit limits the Packers to just 114 total yards for the game (their best mark of the season). After a 5–4 start, the Lions again close like gangbusters to finish 10–4 and earn the NFC wild card berth.

1998 The Cardinals have won just 15 of their last 51 games. The home opener is an unqualified success as they beat the Eagles 17–3. Adrian Murrell is the first Cardinal to rush for more than 100 yards in 30 games (145 on 22 carries). Cardinal pass rushers pour in on the Philadelphia pass pocket the entire game and record 5 sacks. The Cardinals continue on to earn their first play-off berth in 16 years, as they win their final three games of the season to finish 9–7.

The New York Jets have won only 13 of their past 55 games. Curtis Martin records the 1st of his team record forty-three 100-yard rushing performances (144 on 23 carries) in a 44–6 drubbing of the Colts. The Jets gain 505 total yards on offense and begin their drive to their first division title in 29 years (1969). The Bill Parcells–led Jets advance to the AFC title game, where they lose to the defending Super Bowl champion Broncos.

21

1941 League rules in 1941 stated that a touchdown pass will not result in a 1st down, no matter the yardage gained on the play; thus the Packers and Rams combine for just one 1st-down passing in this game. Tailback Tony Canadeo of the Packers throws 18 yards for a 1st-quarter touchdown to Joe Laws. Green Bay completes 4 passes in the game. On a 2nd and 15 play in the 2nd quarter, Canadeo fires to Laws for 12 yards. In the 2nd half on a 1st and 10 play, Hal Van Every completes a toss to Ray Riddick for 9 yards.

Green Bay scores first in the 4th quarter on a 7-yard touchdown toss from Cecil Isbell to future Hall of Famer Clark Hinkle. Marty Slovak of the Rams completes a 48-yard touchdown pass to Johnny Drake late in the 4th quarter. Drake's other reception is for 28 yards on a 3rd and 30 play. The lone 1st down passing comes on a Marty Slovak to Corby Davis completion for 10 yards in the 2nd half.

1969   Mile High Stadium has the largest crowd in Bronco history with 50,583 as the defending Super Bowl champion Jets invade Colorado. New York jumps out to a 13–0 first-quarter lead, but Denver responds with 21 unanswered points on their way to a 21–19 victory. Rookie punter Steve O'Neal of the Jets sets a pro football record with a 98-yard punt as the ball sails over the head of rookie of year Billy Thompson of Denver (Thompson led the AFL in both punt and kickoff returns).

Only five times in their first 118 games did a Bronco rush for more than 100 yards in a game. Floyd Little, with 104 yards against the nasty New York defense, registers his fourth 100-yard game in his last ten games (all victories). This victory is the high point of the season for Denver, while the Jets return to the play-offs.

1986   Dan Marino (30 of 50 for 448 yards) of the Dolphins and Ken O'Brien (29 of 43 for 479 yards) of the Jets combine for 10 touchdown passes in a game that has 7 lead changes. Although Dolphin receivers Mark Duper and Mark Clayton combine for 328 yards receiving on 15 receptions, the receiving hero of the day is Wesley Walker (with 6 catches for 194 yards and 4 TDs) in the Jets 51–45 overtime victory.

22

1940   Green Bay has won the last two Western Conference championships and wins their first game of the season. Veteran lineman Paul "Tiny" Engebretsen kicks a 25-yard field goal to give the Packers an early lead over the visiting Chicago Bears. Rookie George McAfee, in his first league game, returns the kickoff 93 yards for a touchdown. Ray

Nolting of the Bears is awaiting the 2nd-half kickoff with the Bears ahead 14–3. Nolting returns the kick 97 yards for a touchdown, setting a league record. The day belongs to McAfee, however, as he also throws a touchdown pass (to Ken Kavanaugh) and runs for a touchdown in the 41–10 victory. This Bear team continues on to a date with destiny later in the season in our nation's capital.

1963 The defending division champion New York Giants journey to Pittsburgh to take on the resurgent Steelers. The staunch Steeler defense records 8 sacks, and the secondary, led by Pro Bowl strong safety Clendon Thomas, intercepts 4 passes in the 31–0 blowout. New York gains only 175 yards in total offense for the game. Ed Brown throws 2 touchdown passes, including a 46-yard bomb to Buddy Dial in the 4th quarter, yet the offensive juggernaut is future Hall of Fame fullback John Henry Johnson. Johnson gains 123 yards on 24 carries. New York rebounds from the loss and goes on to meet Pittsburgh on the final day of the season to decide the division champion.

1985 The Chargers travel to Cincinnati to play the Bengals. San Diego leads 20–13 at the half, but the Bengals rally to take a 41–34 lead late in the 4th quarter. Dan Fouts and Boomer Esiason both throw for more than 300 yards, yet the star of the game is Lionel "Little Train" James. James gains 127 yards rushing, including a 56-yard 3rd-quarter touchdown run. James gains 118 yards receiving, including a 60-yard reception for the tying touchdown in the 4th quarter. James returns kicks for an additional 71 yards, but he also has a 100-yard kickoff return touchdown called back. Bob Thomas of the Chargers kicks the winning field goal with just four seconds left for a final score of Chargers 44, Bengals 41.

23

1948 We are in Fenway Park on a Thursday evening for a game between the New York Giants and Boston Yanks. We are in the 2nd quarter, and rookie Charley Conerly of the Giants completes a 41-yard pass to George Cheverko (his only reception of the year), who laterals to center Carl Fennema, who goes the remaining 26 yards for a touchdown. It is the 1st of 179 touchdown passes Conerly throws in his long and distinguished Giant career (he continues on to hold the team record until Phil Simms breaks it). New York continues on to win the game, 27–7.

A month later, the Giants are playing the Steelers at the Polo Grounds. Pittsburgh trails 7–6 in the 1st quarter as the Steelers kickoff to Cheverko. After returning the ball 35 yards (the longest kickoff return of his career), Cheverko laterals to offensive tackle Jim White, who weaves his way 54 additional yards for a touchdown. New York goes on to win the game, 34–27.

One week later at Wrigley Field in Chicago, Bears quarterback Johnny Lujack is intercepted by Cheverko. The lateral play has worked twice before, why not again? Cheverko laterals to linebacker John Cannady, who scampers 40 yards but, alas, no touchdown this time as the Bears win, 35–14.

Cheverko is the only player in history to have teammates gain 120 yards on laterals in a season. At this point in the season he is among the leaders in interceptions with 5 and interception return yards with 144, yet he leaves the Giants and finishes the season with the Redskins. To date, the Washington Redskin media guide still lists Cheverko among the seasonal interception return yards with 168, although he intercepted just 1 pass as a Redskin for 24 yards.

1962 The Washington Redskins have won just 3 of their last 36 games, and we are in Cleveland where the Redskins have beaten the Browns just twice in the last 12 years. Future Hall of Famer Bobby Mitchell has caught 2 passes for 44 yards in the game so far, as Washington trails 16–10 in the 4th quarter. Mitchell aligns at right halfback instead of his new position as flanker and releases out of the backfield on a crossing route. He catches Norm Snead's pass at the Browns 40, outruns linebacker Sam Tidmore and right corner Jim Shofner, and cuts dramatically at the sideline. Mitchell gallops up the sideline past his former teammates, cuts back to avoid safeties Don Fleming and Bobby Franklin, and scores the go-ahead points on the 50-yard pass play. In the waning moments of the game, the Redskins block 2 Lou Groza field goal attempts to hang on and win, 17–16. Mitchell goes on to become the first Redskin to ever lead the league in pass receptions (72).

1979 The Buccaneers are the poster children for ineptitude. They have won just 7 of 44 games in their first three seasons. We are in Tampa as the Buccaneers are taking on the Los Angeles Rams (who have won five consecutive Western Division titles). Tampa Bay is trailing 6–0 in the 2nd quarter following a return by Ram linebacker Jim Youngblood off a Doug Williams pass 31 yards for a touchdown. The Buccaneer ground attack controls the clock for the rest of the game as Ricky Bell and Jerry Eckwood grind out 128 yards on 40 attempts. Bell goes on to set team records for attempts (283) and yards rushing in a season (1,263). The Buccaneer defense limits the Rams to 186 yards in total offense in the rain soaked 21–6 victory to remain undefeated at 4–0. Tampa Bay continues on to win their first division title (NFC Central), as their 3–4 defense allows just 85 yards a game rushing in their ten victories, while the Buccaneer ground attack pounds out 197 yards in those ten wins.

24

1950   After their disappointing performance against Otto Graham and Cleveland to open the season, the Eagles rebound by crushing the Cardinals in Chicago 45–7 (it is the first-ever Eagle victory in Chicago against the Cardinals). Cardinal quarterback Jim Hardy has the dubious distinction of setting a league record by throwing 8 interceptions. Russ Craft became the fifth man in league history to intercept 4 passes in a game. Joe Sutton intercepts 3, and former league interception champion Frank Reagan adds the 8th. Philadelphia gains 439 yards total offense. They also record 4 sacks and 12 takeaways as they build a 31–0 halftime lead.

1967   The Cardinals Jim Bakken becomes the first kicker to boot 7 field goals in a game (he attempted 9) in a 28–14 victory over the Steelers in Pittsburgh. For four consecutive years (1964–1967) Bakken finishes in the top two in successful field goals for the season. Bakken led the league in field goal percentage in both 1965 and 1967 (both Pro Bowl seasons). Bakken goes on to score 1,380 points in his 17-year career with the Cardinals.

1972   The Packers are at home and leading the Raiders 7–3 late in the 1st quarter. On 3rd and goal at the 3-yard line, Green Bay running back MacArthur Lane fumbles when hit by Phil Villapiano. All-pro safety Jack Tatum scoops up the loose ball 4 yards deep in the end zone and sets sail for the Packer goal line. The 104-yard fumble return still stands as the record 37 years later. Both the Packers and Raiders go on to the play-offs and lose in the first round.

2000   The 3–0 defending Super Bowl champion Rams are playing the 2–1 Falcons in Atlanta. Torry Holt sets a new record as he averages 63 yards a reception (3 for 189) in a 41–20 Ram victory. Holt scores on an 80-yard reception in the 2nd quarter and an 85 yarder in the 4th quarter. Kurt Warner passes for 336 yards on just 19 attempts. Warner goes on to to set a record with six 300-yard passing games in the season. The Rams continue on to defend their division title but lose in the wild card round of the play-offs against New Orleans.

25

1949   The Chicago Bears have won 18 of their last 24 regular-season games and still do not have a division title to show for it. They open the season on the road against the Packers. The Bears led the league in pass defense efficiency during the 1948 season with a mark of 31.7 and continue their excellent pass defense in this game by setting a league record.

Green Bay attempts 13 passes in the game and completes none. This is the most passes ever attempted in a game without completing a pass. Jug Girard attempts 5 passes in the 2nd quarter (no Packer passer attempts a pass in the 1st quarter) and is intercepted by George McAfee and Bill deCorrevont of the Bears.

Although Chicago moves the ball offensively (the Bears gained 206 yards rushing in the game), the game is scoreless at the half. Girard attempts just 1 pass in the 3rd quarter. Chicago gets on the scoreboard on a Johnny Lujack 16-yard field goal. "Indian Jack" Jacobs attempts 4 passes in the 4th quarter, while Girard's final attempt is intercepted by Jim Canady. Coach Curly Lambeau puts in Stan Heath, who attempts 2 passes, and on the final play of the game Canady intercepts him. Two 4th-quarter touchdown passes by Lujack bring the final score to 17–0.

1988 Bill Walsh is in his tenth and final season as head coach of the 49ers. San Francisco has won 32 of their past 42 road games and is on the road again, this time in Seattle. The Seahawks go on to average 130 yards rushing a game for the season, but today they gain only 29 yards on 12 attempts against San Francisco's multiple-front defense.

Joe Montana completes 20 of 29 passes for 302 yards (his nineteenth 300-yard passing game) and 4 touchdowns. Running back Roger Craig gains 107 yards rushing to key the ground attack. For the second time in his career, Craig gains more than 2,000 yards rushing and receiving.

Jerry Rice catches 6 passes for 163 yards (his fifteenth 100-yard receiving game in his last 35 games) and 3 touchdowns. Montana and Rice strike twice in the 3rd quarter on scoring passes of 69 and 60 yards. The explosive 49er offense gains 580 total yards in the 38–7 victory. For the sixth consecutive season under Walsh, the 49ers earn a play-off berth.

26

1954 The San Francisco 49ers have won 24 of their last 37 games yet do not have a division title to show for their efforts. Is this the year? Reigning league rushing champion

Joe "The Jet" Perry explodes up the middle for 51 yards to set up his own touchdown to start the scoring. Late in the 2nd quarter, larcenous left corner Rex Berry intercepts Redskin Jack Scarbath's sideline pass and gallops 34 yards for a touchdown. Defensive ends Jack Brumfield and Clay Matthews combine for 4 of the 49ers 8 sacks as San Francisco builds up a 34–7 lead late in the 4th quarter. Joe Perry and Hugh McElhenny have combined to gain 144 yards rushing on 21 carries, and now it is rookie John Henry Johnson's turn. On his only carry of the game, he explodes on an inside trap play 8 yards for a touchdown. San Francisco continues on to lead the league in rushing with 2,498 yards (208 a game), as all three future Hall of Fame running backs finish in the top eight in the league in rushing, to no avail, however, as the Lions continue their dominance in the division.

1971   The Dallas Cowboys have won 56 of their last 74 regular-season games but have lost in the play-offs five consecutive years. More than 65,000 Eagle fans pack the Vet in hopes of breaking the seven-game losing streak to Dallas. The Cowboy's offense is led by quarterback Craig Morton (15 of 22 for 188 yards) and Calvin Hill (80 yards rushing on 21 carries), yet this game belongs to "Doomsday." Future Hall of Fame defensive tackle Bob Lilly returns the only Philadelphia fumble 7 yards for a touchdown in the 2nd quarter, the 3rd of his career (still the team record). Future Hall of Fame left corner Herb Adderley intercepts 3, while his teammates grab 4 more. With a 42–0 lead in the 4th quarter, Coach Tom Landry of Dallas elects to attempt a field goal. Al Nelson of the Eagles returns the kick a record-setting 101 yards for the only Philadelphia score.

1976   Rick Upchurch of the Denver Broncos ties a league record as he returns 2 Cleveland punts for a touchdown (73 and 47) in a 44–17 victory.

27

1942   The defending Eastern Conference champion New York Giants open the season in Washington with a field of mud in a driving rainstorm. The Redskins lose their only game of the season, 14–7. Tailback Tuffy Leemans completes just 1 pass the entire game, a 50-yard strike to Will Walls in the 1st quarter. With the score tied at 7 in the 3rd quarter, Dick Poillon's flare pass is intercepted by O'Neal Adams and returned 66 yards for the winning touchdown. The Redskins overcome the loss and win the league title over the undefeated Chicago Bears.

1953   The Baltimore Colt franchise is reborn, and in their first game defensive halfback Bert Rechichar makes history in the 13–9 victory over the visiting Bears. Trailing in the 2nd quarter, Rechichar intercepts future Hall of Famer George Blanda's sideline pass and returns the ball 36 yards for a touchdown. Later in the 2nd quarter, Rechichar attempts the first field goal of his career and splits the uprights from 56 yards. He is the only player in league history to return an interception for a touchdown and kick a 50-yard field goal in the same quarter. Although the Colts gain only 164 yards in total offense, the Baltimore defense is the difference with 8 takeaways. Besides Rechichar's 3 interceptions, Pro Bowl safety Tom Keane records the 1st of his team record 11 interceptions.

1970   The Minnesota Vikings shut out the Saints 26–0 to improve their record to 2–0. The "Purple Gang" allows a season best of just 131 yards in total offense to the Saints. Besides Fred Cox's 4 field goals, the 2 touchdowns by Minnesota come via the defense (Mike McGill's 5-yard fumble return in the 4th quarter) and special teams (Ed "Bozo" Sharockman's end zone recovery of a blocked punt). Sharockman is the only Viking in team history to return 2 blocked punts for a touchdown in a season. Sharockman is part of a secondary that ranks first in the defensive passer rating with a mark of 40.4 and a defense that allows just 4 rushing touchdowns all season. Minnesota defends their division title and returns to the play-offs for the third consecutive season.

28

1951 The Rams are opening the season in the Coliseum against the New York Yanks on a Friday evening. Norm Van Brocklin goes the distance at quarterback for Los Angeles (he usually rotated by quarters with Bob Waterfield). After 3 quarters, Van Brocklin has gained 393 yards passing on 17 completions and 4 touchdowns as the Rams lead 41–7. Van Brocklin keeps passing and finishes with a record (which still stands) of 554 yards passing. Verda "Vitamin T" Smith, Tom Fears, and Elroy Hirsch combine to catch 18 passes for 438 yards and all 5 receiving touchdowns (all three men gain more than 100 yards receiving) in the 54–14 victory. Waterfield (81.8) and Van Brocklin (80.8) finish the season as the two most efficient passers in the league. Los Angeles also ranks first in total offense with 5,409 yards (450 yards a game). The Rams survive a four-team battle to win their conference title and earn a rematch with Cleveland for the championship.

1969 The 0–1 defending NFL champion Colts are at the Met to play the 0–1 Vikings. The result of this game will be far different than last year's Western Conference play-off game. Minnesota quarterback Joe Kapp has thrown 18 touchdown passes in his 27-game career entering this season, but today he becomes just the fifth player to throw 7 touchdown passes in a game. Kapp completes 28 of 43 passes for 449 yards (the eighth best total in league history) in the 52–14 victory. Six different receivers catch touchdown passes (Gene Washington catches 2). Minnesota gains 622 yards in total offense (which still stands as the team record). The Viking defense allows Baltimore just 56 yards rushing and intercepts 3 Colt passes. In Viking lore, this special group of men is forever known as "40 for 60," led by Joe Kapp.

29

1968 After competing for the Eastern Division title during the 1963 and 1964 seasons, the Cardinals have won just 19 of their last 44 games. St. Louis is in New Orleans and trails 17–0 entering the 4th quarter. Tom McNeil of the Saints punts to Chuck Latourette, who fields the ball near the right hash on his own 14. Latourette weaves his way to the left, twists out of Tony Lorick's tackle, and gets to the sideline, and 86 yards later the Cardinals are back in a game they eventually win, 21–20. Latourette sets a league record for punt return average in a game as he returns 3 punts for 143 yards. He also sets a season record for combined kick return yards with 1,582. St. Louis continues on to win 9 of their last 12 games, yet falls just short of a division title.

1974 We are at War Memorial Stadium with gusting winds and heavy rain. The Bills trail 12–10 entering the 4th quarter, but their powerful ground attack pounds away until Jim Braxton breaks free on a 21-yard run (behind a crushing Joe DeLamielleure block). They win the game 16–12. Buffalo quarterback Joe Ferguson attempts just 2 passes (both incomplete), while the Jets Joe Namath throws 3 interceptions. Namath completes 2 (Willie Brister and David Knight) of 8 attempts, setting a modern-day record of just 2 completed passes in a game. The Buffalo Bills continue their winning ways and earn a play-off berth (wild card) for the first time since 1966.

1985 The Cowboys are on the road and tied at 10 entering the 4th quarter against the Oilers. Tony Dorsett provides the punch in the Dallas ground game with 159 yards on 23 carries. The Dallas defense is the difference in the game as they intercept future Hall of Fame quarterback Warren Moon 4 times. Nine men provide relentless pressure on Moon as the Cowboys set a team record with 12 sacks. Danny White's 1-yard touchdown pass to Fred Cornwell is the winning score with just over a minute left. This team proves to be Tom Landry's last division champion.

30

1973 The defending AFC Central champion Pittsburgh Steelers are in Houston to play an Oiler team that has won just 6 of their last 41 games. Trailing 7–6 entering the 3rd quarter, the Steeler defense takes control of the game as right outside linebacker Andy Russell returns an interception 45 yards for a touchdown, and late in the 4th quarter free safety Glen Edwards returns an interception 86 yards for a touchdown (the second time in team history that the Steelers have returned 2 interceptions for a touchdown in a game), as Pittsburgh wins 36–7.

The Steelers go on to lead the league in the defensive passer rating with a mark of 33.1, becoming the most efficient team pass defense in 50 years. Pittsburgh earns a wild card berth in the play-offs. The Oilers, however, will again win just 1 of 14 games.

1984 The revitalized Rams are at home to play the Giants before a crowd of 53,417. Eric Dickerson, on his way to setting a record for most yards gained rushing in his first two years in the league, gallops for 120 yards. Leading 17–6 in the 3rd quarter, the Ram defense tackles Phil Simms in the end zone for a safety and blocks 2 punts out of the end zone for safeties, thus a league record that still exists today of 3 safeties in a single game. Los Angeles limits the Giants to just 8 yards rushing on 13 attempts in the 33–12 victory. Both the Giants and Rams earn wild card berths in the play-offs and meet again in Anaheim in a rematch.

The Buccaneers have a workhorse fullback in James Wilder, who carried the ball a record-setting 42 times in a game in 1983, only to have the record broken later in the season by Butch Woolfolk. In the 1st half at home against Green Bay, Wilder carries 22 times for 112 yards (including a 33-yard TD run). Then in the 2nd half, Wilder carries 17 times for 38 yards, and the Bucs lead 27–20. Lynn Dickey, of the Packers, completes a pass to James Lofton, who laterals to Gerry Ellis for the tying touchdown with eight seconds left. In overtime, Wilder carries 4 more times to tie the record (43) and gains 22 yards to set up the winning field goal.

October

1

1961 The distance between Dallas and Detroit is about 1,000 miles in a straight line, yet today the games played in these cities are eerily the same. Let us first go to Tiger Stadium. Coaches Howard "Red" Hickey and George Wilson competed against each other on the field of play 20 years earlier (Rams versus Bears). San Francisco and Detroit tied for the division title in 1957 and for second place in 1960.

The 2–0 first-place Lions begin the game with Earl Morrall being intercepted by Pro Bowl right corner Abe Woodson of the 49ers. The 49ers open the game in their spread formation ("shotgun") and drive 59 yards in 5 plays to score on a wing left sweep right by J. D. Smith from the 5-yard line. Late in the 1st quarter, a 91-yard drive is culminated in a 10-yard sweep left by tailback Bobby Waters.

Detroit, down 21–0, kicks off to open the 2nd half to Abe Woodson, who takes the ball on his 2-yard line, sprints up the middle of the field to his own 38, spins, cuts left, then hurdles a teammate at the Lion 30, and continues up the sideline to score. The rest of the 3rd quarter is marred by Lion turnovers. Left safety Dave Baker intercepts twice (setting up tailback Billy Kilmer's 7-yard run and stopping a Lion drive). Leo "The Lion" Nomellini recovers a fumble on the Detroit 2, and again left wing J. D. Smith powers in over right tackle. Rookie and future Hall of Famer Jimmy Johnson records the 1st interception of his career as San Francisco wins, 49–0.

Nine times in the last nine years a 49er has recorded a 100-yard rushing game against Detroit, and today it is tailback Billy Kilmer with the first of his three consecutive 100-yard games (103 on 16 carries). Yet it is the play by play of the game that speaks volumes: "Waters ran through a hole on the left side at least 15 feet wide."

Now to Dallas, where the Texans set a league record with 398 yards rushing against the defending league champion Oilers. For the first time in AFL history, teammates both gain 100 yards rushing as Jack Spikes (146 on 15) and Abner Haynes (117 on 19) go the distance and score 4 times in building a 26–7 lead (eventually winning 26–21). Although Dallas and Houston combine to gain 502 rushing (a league record), it is the power attack out of varied formations by Dallas that highlights the game. The tough Texan defense contributes 5 turnovers to the cause.

2

1950 Welcome to Monday night football. The Chicago Cardinals are hoping to rebound from the embarrassing loss to the Eagles as they host the Baltimore Colts at Comiskey Park. Bob Shaw makes a fine over-the-shoulder 40-yard touchdown reception in the 1st quarter to give the Cardinals the lead. Trailing 13–7 in the 3rd quarter, Shaw, aligned at tight end right, catches a 9-yard pass from Jim

Hardy at the backline of the end zone. Later in the quarter, Shaw makes a juggling catch in the right corner of the end zone for 19 yards and a touchdown. Shaw is wide open in the middle of the end zone for an 18-yard 4th-quarter touchdown. Hardy lofts a pass to Shaw, who outleaps the Colt defenders for 28 yards and his record-setting 5th touchdown reception in the 55–13 Cardinal victory. In the last game of the 1949 season, Shaw (playing for the Rams) had tied Don Hutson's record with 4 touchdown receptions in a game. Shaw goes on to play only 38 games in his career.

1966 The 3-0 Cardinals are on the road to take on the 2-1 Philadelphia Eagles in a battle of Eastern Division contenders. Leading 7-0 in the 1st quarter, rookie of the year Johnny Roland of the Cardinals fields Sam Baker's punt at his own 14. Roland heads up the sideline behind picket blocking and then cuts back at the Eagle 40 and outruns Tom Woodeshick. St. Louis goes on to a 41-10 victory.

Roland sets a team record for punt return average, as he returns 3 punts for 143 yards (47.6). Leading 27-10 entering the 4th quarter, strong safety Jerry Stovall intercepts a Norm Snead pass and goes 18 yards for a touchdown. Not to be outdone, free safety Larry Wilson makes a one-handed interception on a pass to Timmy Brown, scrambles to his feet, and legs it 91 yards for the final score (the Cardinals intercept 5 passes in the game). Pro Bowl defensive tackle Chuck Walker leads a Cardinal pass rush that records 9 sacks on a day when the Cardinal offense manages only 147 yards in total offense.

1983 The 2-2 Rams defeat the Lions 21-10 at home, as rookie talent Eric Dickerson continues to lug the leather.

He has gained 391 yards rushing in his last two games on 58 carries, as he goes on to set rookie rushing records for the play-off bound (9–7) John Robinson–led Rams.

3

1971   The 0–2 Buffalo Bills travel to the Met to play the 1–1 Minnesota Vikings. In their last 46 regular-season games, the Vikings have allowed just 50 offensive touchdowns (16 rushing and 34 passing). Minnesota sets a team record by allowing Buffalo just 64 yards in total offense. Bills quarterback Dennis Shaw completes 12 of 20 for 67 yards, but he is sacked 7 times for 59 yards by the "Purple Gang" and, as such, the 8 yards allowed passing are also a team record.

Viking running backs Clint Jones and Dave Osborn gain 275 yards rushing and receiving to provide the offense. In the 2nd quarter, league MVP and future Hall of Famer Alan Page forces Shaw to fumble the ball out of the end zone for a safety and a 12–0 halftime lead. Minnesota continues their record-setting pace defensively in the 19–0 victory.

1976   The 2–0–1 Rams journey to the Orange Bowl to take on the 2–1 Dolphins. Miami gains 219 yards rushing and leads 14–0 at the half. Los Angeles quarterback James Harris completes 17 of 29 passes for 436 yards (he is the third Ram passer to throw for more than 400 yards in a game) and 2 touchdowns to rally the Rams with the help of receiver Ron Jessie (220 yards on 7 catches).

When Ram running back Lawrence McCutcheon (91 yards on 22 carries) scores from the 9-yard line in the 4th quarter, the Rams have the lead at 28–21. Miami comes back and scores on a Bob Griese to Nat Moore 47-yard pass. Harris throws deep to Harold Jackson for 50 yards just before the two-minute warning, putting the Rams on the Dolphin 10-yard line. Los Angeles wins the game on Tom Dempsey's 19-yard field goal.

1999 The 1–2 Panthers are on the road to play the 2–1 Redskins. Tshimanga Biakabutuka gains 123 yards rushing in the 1st quarter on just 5 carries and scores 3 times (60, 1, and 45). Panther quarterback Steve Beuerlein completes 23 passes for 334 yards, as Carolina sets a team record with 483 yards in total offense. Washington rallies behind the accurate passing of Brad Johnson, who completes 20 of 33 for 337 yards and 4 touchdowns to take a 35–27 lead. Carolina scores the first 9 points in the 4th quarter but the Redskins win on a late Brett Conway field goal, 38–36.

4

1958 Washington coach Joe Kuharich, in his final season, brings his Redskins to Comiskey Park on a Saturday evening to play the Cardinals under new coach "Pop" Ivy. The Cardinals, in their new look double-wing offense, explode for a season high in rushing (261) and total offense (531) in the 37–10 victory.

Rookie John David Crow, aligned at right wing, scores on the longest run in Cardinal history with an 83-yard trap left to get Chicago rolling in the 1st quarter. After another Crow scoring run, his college teammate rookie defensive halfback/kicker Bobby Joe Conrad adds an 18-yard field goal as Chicago leads 17–0 at the half. Cardinal quarterback Lamar McHan, with a 30–10 4th-quarter lead, fires a strike to future Hall of Famer Ollie Matson, who is aligned at left wing for 51 yards on a post pattern and the final score of the game. Chicago continues on to win just once more all season.

1964 The 3–0 defending Eastern Division champion Boston Patriots travel to Mile High Stadium in Denver to take on the 0–3 Broncos. AFL all-star Gino Cappelletti sets a pro football record as he kicks 6 field goals in 6 attempts in one game (Roger LeClerc and Lou Groza had 5). Cappelletti's 6 field goals are in the first 3 quarters of the game, as Boston builds a 25–0 lead. The punishing Patriot defense allows Denver only 53 yards rushing and averages giving up just 82 yards a game all season.

Boston bruiser Larry Eisenhauer leads a pass rush that records 8 sacks, while safety Ron Hall records 1 of his 11 interceptions on the season. In their last 24 games, the Patriots have had just one 100-yard rusher, but today halfback J. D. Garrett pounds out 121 yards on 12 carries to key the offense.

The Cardinals have won 13 of their past 19 games and are visiting Washington, where coach Bill McPeak brings his revamped (only 19 players return from the 1963 roster) Redskins into battle. Pro Bowl left corner Pat Fischer gets St. Louis on the board first with a 33-yard interception return early in the 1st quarter. Right defensive end Don Brumm leads a Cardinal pass rush that registers 9 sacks in the 23–17 victory. Split end Sonny Randle catches 5 passes for 139 yards to key an offense that gains 454 total yards.

5

1947 The New York Giants have beaten the Eagles 19 of the 26 times they have played entering this game. Philadelphia is at home coming off their high-scoring victory over the Redskins. Earle "Greasy" Neale's defense has come to play, as the Giants gain just 39 yards on the ground in shutting out New York, 23–0 (just their second shutout of the Giants). Philadelphia allows just 80 yards rushing a game in their eight victories.

The Eagle ground game is in fine form as future Hall of Famer Steve Van Buren gains 105 yards on 16 carries (the third time he has gained 100 rushing against New York). Van Buren goes on to win the rushing title and becomes just the second runner in league history to gain more than 1,000 yards in a season, as Philadelphia earns their first division title.

1952 For the second consecutive week, the Dallas Texans discover just how difficult it is to stop powerful NFL ground attacks. They have surrendered 532 yards (81 attempts) in losses to the Giants and 49ers at home. The Texans rank dead last in run defense as they allow 2,334 yards for the season, even with Art Donovan and Gino Marchetti.

The "King" has arrived, as Hugh McElhenny gains 170 yards rushing on just 7 carries, including an 89-yard excursion through the Texan defense. McElhenny catches just 1 pass in the game (33 yards for a touchdown in the 4th quarter) and returns kickoffs and punts for 46 yards. On just 11 touches he gains 249 yards.

Defensive halfbacks Lowell Wagner and Rex Berry blanket the Texan receivers, resulting in Dallas completing just 6 of 23 for 59 yards.

1980 The 1–3 Cardinals are in the Superdome to play the 0–4 Saints. The Cardinals 3–4 defense stymies the Saint ground game as they gain just 15 yards (9 attempts) and 80 yards in total offense, while St. Louis gains a season high with 433 total yards (330 rushing). For just the second time in team history, teammates both gain more than 100 rushing (Wayne Morris with 102 on 22 carries and O. J. Anderson with 126 on 22 carries) in the 40–7 victory. The only score from New Orleans comes on a blocked punt return.

6

1963 We are at Tiger Stadium in Detroit for the continuing rivalry of the 49ers and Lions. In the past 13 years, each team has won 13 times in many a classic battle. Former Lion great Jack Christiansen returns to a site of many of his greatest games, but now he is the coach of San Francisco (his first game as head coach).

Although "Williams, Walker, and Watkins" sounds like a law firm, they are in fact the key men in this record-setting game. San Francisco passers gain only 63 yards passing on 10 completions but lose 73 yards as they are sacked by Lion pass rushers, thus the third best pass defensive performance in Detroit history (–10 yards). San Francisco gains just 71 yards rushing (only 5 in the 2nd half) for a total offense of 61 yards, the fourth best total defensive performance in Detroit history.

Right outside linebacker Wayne Walker (2 sacks) and right defensive end Sam Williams (3½ sacks) lead the silver and blue charge into the 49er backfield. In the 1st quarter, Tommy Davis punts to Tommy Watkins, who returns the ball 26 yards. Later in the quarter, Watkins returns a Davis punt 90 yards for a touchdown (a new Lion record). In the 2nd half, Watkins returns punts for 9 and 16 yards. Finally, late in the 4th quarter Watkins takes Davis's punt on his own 41, and to quote the play by play: "miraculously writhing out of the arms of six tacklers, returned 43 yards and stumbled and fell all by himself" on the 49er 16-yard line. Watkins sets a new league record for punt return yardage in a game with 184. Defense and special teams are the difference in the 26–3 victory.

1974   Future Hall of Famer Bobby Bell is about to play in his 158th consecutive game as a Chief (he never misses a game in his 12-year career). Bell has demonstrated big play ability his entire career, and today will be no different. In his last game against the Broncos at Municipal Stadium, Bell returns a 2nd-quarter interception 28 yards for a touchdown to give the Chiefs a 14–3 lead. He has now returned 6 interceptions for a touchdown in his career (the most by a linebacker in league history).

7

1934   The 2–0 Lions are in Green Bay at East Stadium to play the 2–1 Packers. In the 2nd quarter, Glenn Presnell of the Lions kicks a record-setting 54-yard field goal in a 3–0 Detroit victory.

1945   The 1–0 Lions are at City Stadium to play the 0–1 Packers. Don Hutson is playing his final season and as such has established a boatload of records, yet today is possibly his greatest. Hutson catches 4 touchdown passes in the 2nd quarter and scores 29 points (a league record). He catches 6 passes for 144 yards (the first of his only four-consecutive game streak of 100 yards receiving). Roy McKay throws 4 of his 6 career touchdown passes (he attempts only 103 passes in his career). The Packers intercept 6 passes (Ted Fritsch and Charley Brock return theirs for touchdowns) in the 57–21 victory.

1949 The 0–2 Packers are in New York to play the 0–2 Bulldogs on a Friday night. Green Bay gains a season high 385 yards, while the Bulldogs gain just 189 (the fewest the Packers allow all year) in a 19–0 victory. Future Hall of Famer Tony Canadeo gains 94 of his 100 yards (16 carries) in the 2nd half to key the victory. His 27-yard run, followed by Walt Schlinkman's 37-yard run, positions the Packers for Ted Fritsch's 14-yard field goal in the 3rd quarter. Late in the 4th quarter, Canadeo scores on a 15-yard touchdown run (he carried 5 times on the drive). Canadeo goes on to gain more than 100 yards rushing (the team record until Jim Taylor in 1960) five times during the season.

1956 The 0–1 Bears are at East Stadium in Green Bay to play the 0–1 Packers. After a Rick Casares touchdown, Al Carmichael returns the Bear kickoff 106 yards for a touchdown (a record that stands until 2007) in a 37–21 Chicago victory.

1990 The 3–1 Bengals are at Anaheim Stadium to play the 1–2 Rams. Boomer Esiason sets a team record by passing for 490 yards (he completes 31 of 45) for 3 touchdowns in the Bengals 34–31 overtime victory. Five men gain more than 100 yards receiving: Rodney Holman, James Brooks, and Tim McGee for Cincinnati and Henry Ellard and Flipper Anderson for the Rams.

8

1933 Fenway Park is the site of the home opener for the Boston Redskins, as they take on the Giants. Halfback Cliff

Battles sets the league record for most yards gained rushing in a game with 215 (on just 16 carries) in a 21–20 victory. Since Battles gained 115 yards rushing the week before against Pittsburgh, he is the also the first player in league history to gain more than 300 yards in a two-game span (31 for 330). Battles continues on to finish second in rushing for the season with 737, behind teammate Jim Musick (809).

1939 The Chicago Cardinals are at Wisconsin State Fair Park in Milwaukee to play the defending league champion Green Bay Packers. Don Hutson records the longest touchdown reception of his career (92 yards) to put Green Bay ahead 7–0 in the 1st quarter. Leading 14–0 in the 3rd quarter, halfback Andy Uram of the Packers breaks free on the longest run from scrimmage in league history to go 97 yards for a touchdown. Uram gains 108 yards for the day on just 2 carries in the Packers 27–20 victory. Green Bay returns to the championship game.

1950 Billy Grimes of the Packers sets the record for highest average per carry in a game in a 44–31 loss to the New York Yanks, as he gains 167 yards on just 10 carries. By this point in the season, Grimes has returned 10 punts for 237 yards, and he goes on to set a new league record for punt return yards in a season with 555 (he holds the record for 17 years). Billy also establishes a new record for combined kick return yards in a season with 1,155 and most net yards in a season with 1,896.

1961 Paul Hornung scores a team record 33 points in a 45–7 victory over the Colts at City Stadium in Green Bay. Hornung gains 111 yards rushing on just 11 carries, including a 54-yard touchdown run in the 1st quarter, to get the Packer engine started. Hornung scores 4 touchdowns, kicks a 2nd-quarter field goal, and earns 6 extra points. He has scored 240 points in his last 16 games and goes on to lead the league in scoring again as Green Bay returns to the championship game.

9

1938 At home at Forbes Field, the 2–3 Pittsburgh Pirates host the 1–1–1 Brooklyn Dodgers. Leading 10–7 in the 4th quarter, future Hall of Famer Clarence "Ace" Parker breaks off a 77-yard run for the clinching touchdown in a 17–7 win. Parker gains 103 yards rushing on 15 carries in the game, while Pirate rookie Byron "Whizzer" White records the first 100-yard rushing performance in the history of the franchise, as he totals 116 yards on 16 carries. White goes on to lead the league with 567 yards rushing (152 attempts). It is the first time in league history that a player from each team gains more than 100 yards rushing.

1966 The 3–0 Cowboys are in the Cotton Bowl to face division rival Philadelphia. Dallas sets team records for largest margin of victory (49), most points scored (56), and total yards gained (652) in the win. Pro Bowl quarterback Don Meredith ties his team record of throwing 5 touchdown passes in a game, as he completes 19 of 26 for 394 yards (the second most in team history at that time). His main target is future Hall of Fame split end Bob Hayes, who catches 6 passes for 107 yards and a team tying record of 3 touchdown receptions in a game. For the first time in team history, the Cowboys win four in a row, and they are on their way to their first division title.

1977 The Dallas Cowboys have won 31 of their past 40 regular-season games and are in St. Louis to play the Cardinals. St. Louis and Dallas split their last six games, and the Cardinals lead 17–16 in the 3rd quarter when Charles Davis of St. Louis lumbers 35 yards with a Roger Staubach fumble to increase the lead.

Entering the game rookie Tony Dorsett had carried the ball just 21 times in three games (he gained 145 yards); today he tallies the first 100-yard rushing performance of his Hall of Fame career (141 yards on 14 carries). Dorsett broke loose on a 77-yard touchdown run in the 2nd quarter and, now in the 4th quarter, he plunges for a touchdown to cut the Cardinal lead to 1. Fourth-quarter interceptions by Cowboy safeties Cliff Harris and Charlie Waters stop Cardinal drives, and with seven minutes to play Staubach hits Golden Richards with a 17-yard winning touchdown pass.

10

1934 The defending league champion Bears are on the road for the fourth consecutive week to play the Pirates on a Wednesday night at Forbes Field. Chicago's 28–0 victory is part of a streak in which the Bears have lost just 2 of their past 26 regular-season games and are undefeated so far in the season.

Rookie halfback Beattie Feathers gains more than 100 yards rushing for the third consecutive game (in just 11 days) on just 8 carries. In those three games, he gained 373 yards on 40 carries. Feathers scores on an 82-yard spectacular touchdown run in the 2nd quarter to put Chicago ahead, 14–0. Feathers goes on to become the league's first 1,000-yard rusher, as the Bears return to the championship game.

1954   New York has a new head coach in Jim Lee Howell and a new offensive coordinator in Vince Lombardi. The 0–2 Washington Redskins are playing host to the 1–1 Giants (their third straight road game). The 1953 Giants finished dead last in rushing and gain 166 yards today on their way to an improved seventh-place finish in yards rushing for the 1954 season. Bob Schnelker ties a team record with 3 touchdowns on his 8 catches for 136 yards. The Giant defense is led by a future Hall of Fame safety Emlen Tunnell and player/coach and future Hall of Famer Tom Landry. Tunnell registers 1 of his record-setting 15 interceptions against the Redskins in the 51–21 victory (the most points New York has ever scored on Washington at this point in the rivalry).

1964   It is Saturday night in Cleveland, as the 3–0–1 Browns take on the 2–2 Steelers before more than 80,000 fans. Fullback John Henry Johnson becomes just the 12th man in the last 32 years to gain at least 200 yards rushing in a game. Johnson is the first man, though, to gain 200 yards rushing against the season league champion. He scores twice in the 1st half on runs of 33 and 45 yards to stake the Steelers to a 16–7 lead. He scores again in the 3rd quarter to sew up the 23–7 win. Pittsburgh uses a five-man defensive line, with nickle coverage for the entire game, and Jim Brown is limited to just 59 yards rushing.

11

1942   We are at Ebbets Field to witness the 2–0 Brooklyn Dodgers host the 1–2 Pittsburgh Steelers. This game features the two men who will rank first and second in rushing for the season in future Hall of Famer Bill Dudley (696) and former Pittsburgh Pirate Merlyn "The Magician" Condit (647).

The Dodgers, in their two victories, gained 333 yards rushing on 82 carries, but today the stalwart Steeler defense limits them to 86 yards on 36 attempts. Rookie Bill Dudley scores the only touchdown of the game on a 7-yard run in the 7–0 victory. Dudley also contributes an interception return of 25 yards for the defense. The Steelers allow only 33 points in their next seven games (winning six). The Steelers remain the only team in the last 70 years to not throw a touchdown pass in victory during a winning season.

1981   The 3–2 Kansas City Chiefs are at home against the 2–3 defending Super Bowl champion Raiders. Courageous Pro Bowl running back Joe Delaney, in his first start, gains 106 rushing and 104 receiving (only the third player in franchise history to accomplish this feat) as the Chiefs shut out the Raiders for the first time in 43 meetings 27–0. Oakland's best opportunity to score is just before the half, but Pro Bowl safety Gary Barbaro's interception stops the drive to keep the shutout alive. The Raiders are the first team to be shut out three consecutive weeks since the 1943 Brooklyn Dodgers.

1998   The 5–0 defending Super Bowl champion Denver Broncos are on the road in Seattle to play the 3–2 Seahawks. The Bronco running game is still in high gear as Terrell Davis gains 208 yards rushing on 30 carries (his fifth consecutive 100-yard game) in the 21–16 victory. Denver continues on to lead the AFC in both rushing and scoring, and led by Davis and his offensive line, they return to the play-offs. Davis becomes just the fourth man to gain more than 2,000 yards rushing in a season, as he leads the league with 2,008. More importantly, Denver, with this victory, is 22–3 (at this point in Davis's career) in games where Davis rushes for more than 100 yards.

12

1952 Who can dethrone the champion Rams? The two main contenders for the conference title square off in Detroit. The 2–0 49ers put a stranglehold on the Lion offense, which gains just 65 yards on 48 offensive plays. San Francisco allows just four 1st downs to set a team defensive record that stands for 21 years.

Future Hall of Fame running backs Joe "The Jet" Perry and Hugh "The King" McElhenny combine to gain 136 yards rushing on 32 carries (Detroit allowed only 95 yards a game rushing all season). Y. A. Tittle is an efficient 13 of 18 for 90 yards passing as San Francisco builds a 21–0 3rd-quarter lead.

Future Hall of Fame quarterback Bobby Layne completes just 5 of 15 for 43 yards. Lion passers are sacked 5 times for 49 yards, and the Leo "The Lion" Nomellini–led D-line stonewalls the Detroit ground game, which gains just 40 yards on 17 carries. San Francisco linebacker Don Burke returns an interception 35 yards for a touchdown in the 4th quarter, and the victory is complete. San Francisco registers their first shutout in NFL history, 28–0.

1958 The 1–1 Chicago Cardinals are in Cleveland to take on the 2–0 defending conference champion Browns. Future Hall of Famers Jim Brown and rookie Bobby Mitchell gain 329 yards rushing on 45 carries in the 35–28 victory. It is the second time in team history teammates have rushed for more than 100 yards apiece in a game. Since joining the NFL, the Browns record when having a 100-yard rusher is 23–1.

Leading 14–7 in the 2nd quarter, Mitchell sweeps right behind an exceptional open field block by Jim Ray Smith and high steps 63 yards for a touchdown. Brown scores from 7 yards out in the 4th quarter for his 3rd touchdown of the game to give Cleveland a 35–14 lead. Rookie John David Crow catches 2 touchdown passes later in the 4th quarter (1 for 91 yards).

1997 The 3–3 Detroit Lions defeat the 5–1 Buccaneers in Tampa 27–9 behind Barry Sanders's 215 yards rushing. Sanders scores on touchdown runs of 80 (1st quarter) and 82 (3rd quarter), as he notches his second 200-yard rushing game against the Bucs in his career. He goes on to become just the third man to rush for more than 2,000 yards in a season (2,053). Detroit continues on to meet Tampa in the play-offs.

13

1961 The defending league champion Oilers are on the road to play the Patriots. Houston has lost three straight, yet Charley Hennigan has gained 319 receiving yards on 13 catches in those games. With the score tied at 7 in the 2nd quarter, Jackie Lee finds Hennigan open for 48 yards and the go-ahead touchdown. Hennigan becomes just the fourth man to gain more than 250 yards receiving in a game as he catches 13 passes for 272 yards in the 31-all tie with Boston. During the 1961 season, Hennigan sets records for yards receiving in a season with 1,746 and consecutive games with more than 100 yards receiving with seven.

1985 The 3–2 Giants take on the 1–4 Bengals at River-front Stadium. Quarterback Phil Simms becomes just the fourth man to pass for more than 500 yards in a game. Cincinnati leads 21–3 at the half, and the New York running game is not proving productive. Simms just keeps throwing and sets team records for attempts (62), completions (40), and yards (513).

Late in the 3rd quarter, the Giants have cut the Bengal lead to 21–20 and have the ball. James Griffin of Cincinnati returns a Simms interception 24 yards for a touchdown, and linebacker Reggie Williams forces a Simms fumble that becomes a Rodney Holman 5-yard touchdown reception. Simms continues to find Lionel Manuel (8 receptions for 111 yards) and Mark Bavaro (12 receptions for 176 yards) open as the Giants continue to rally. New York scores the last 10 points of the game but loses 35–30.

2002 The 4–1 New Orleans Saints are on the road to play the 2–2 Washington Redskins. The Redskins trail 20–7 and kickoff to Michael Lewis of the Saints, who returns the ball 90 yards for a touchdown. Washington trails 29–21 in the 3rd quarter and punts to Lewis, who returns the ball 83 yards for a touchdown (he is the seventh man to return a punt and kickoff for a touchdown in the same game). Lewis gains 356 combined net yards in the game on just 8 opportunities in the 43–27 New Orleans victory.

14

1951 Two future Hall of Fame left safeties will both go on to break the record for most punt return yards on the same day. We are at the Polo Grounds to watch the 1–1 Cardinals take on the 1–0–1 Giants. Trailing 10–7 in the

2nd quarter, Emlen Tunnell returns a Cardinal punt 81 yards for the longest punt return in team history and the go-ahead score. New York turns the ball over 8 times (safety Ray Ramsey of Chicago records his league-leading 5th interception), yet the Giants win.

Two-way halfback Don Paul of the Cardinals catches his 2nd touchdown pass of the half (he also intercepts in the game), and Chicago leads at the half, 17–14. Tunnell sets up Eddie Price's 25-yard scoring run with another of his patented change-of-pace weaving returns in the 4th quarter as New York goes on to win, 28–17. Tunnell gains 147 yards on 4 punt returns. Meanwhile, in Detroit the 2–0 first-place Lions are hosting the defending conference champion 1–1 Rams at Briggs Stadium. Detroit trails 10–7 in the 2nd quarter, when Norm Van Brocklin punts to rookie Jack Christiansen, who "proceeds to dance, weave, wriggle, and slice his way through tackler after tackler, finally breaking loose to run wide along the East sideline for a 69-yard touchdown."

In the 4th quarter, the Rams lead 27–14, and again Van Brocklin punts to Christiansen. Christiansen goes 47 yards to become the first man in league history to return 2 punts for a touchdown in the same game (he will remarkably repeat this feat later in the season). Hall of Fame quarterbacks Norm Van Brocklin and Bob Waterfield complete 16 of 32 for 272 yards and 3 touchdowns. Future Hall of Famer Elroy Hirsch catches 7 for 146 yards to provide the difference in the 27–21 win.

2007 The 1–3 Vikings are at Soldier Field to battle the 2–3 Bears. Rookie Adrian Peterson gains 224 yards rushing on 20 carries; however, and even more impressive, he is the only Bear opponent ever to score on 3 touchdown runs of

35 yards or longer (he also scores on runs of 67 and 73 yards) in the same game. Peterson sets a team record with 361 combined net yards in the 34–31 Minnesota victory (his 53-yard kickoff return sets up the winning 4th-quarter field goal).

15

1922   The Rock Island Independents defeat the Evansville Crimson Giants (they will play only three games), 60–0. Future Hall of Famer Jimmy Conzelman is the first player in pro football history to score 5 touchdowns in a game (all rushing).

1967   The 2–2 revitalized Houston Oilers journey to Shea Stadium to take on the 3–1 New York Jets. The Oilers manage to gain only 131 yards in total offense, yet they are able to tie the Jets 28 all. Joe Namath throws for 295 yards on his 27 completions, and his main target, Don Maynard, catches 10 passes for 157 yards and a 2nd-quarter touchdown to give the Jets a 14–0 lead.

Rookie Ken Houston returns a blocked field goal attempt 71 yards for a touchdown and returns a Namath interception 43 yards for a touchdown in the 3rd quarter to give the Oilers a 28–20 lead. Cornerback Miller Farr intercepts 3 passes and returns them 128 yards, including a 51-yard touchdown return in the 3rd quarter, to start the Oiler rally. Houston returns the 6 interceptions off of Namath an AFL record-setting 245 yards. New York ties the game in the 4th quarter, but a three-game losing streak late in the season costs them the division title to the Oilers.

The 3–0–1 defending Super Bowl champion Packers are at Lambeau Field to play the winless Vikings and their new coach, Bud Grant. The "Purple Gang" limits Green Bay to just 42 yards rushing (fewest of the season), and when Fred Cox kicks a 12-yard field goal in the 4th quarter, Bud Grant has his first victory as head coach of the Vikings. As well, he defeats Vince Lombardi in his final season as Packers coach, 10–7.

1972 The 3–1 Redskins journey to St. Louis to play the 2–2 Cardinals. Washington limits the Cardinals to 66 yards rushing, while their ground game is in high gear with league MVP Larry Brown. He gains 110 on 23 carries (his fourth of six 100-yard rushing performances on the season). Washington cornerbacks Pat Fischer and Mike Bass intercept and Curt Knight kicks 4 field goals in the 33–3 victory.

16

1966 The expansion 0–5 Miami Dolphins are at home against the 1–4 Denver Broncos. Miami has allowed 165 points in their five losses; however, today is the day of the defense, as led by AFL all-stars Willie West, Tom Erlandson, and Ed Cooke. The Dolphins allow just 118 yards in total offense (a team record for 97 games) and record 5 sacks and 6 takeaways in their first-ever victory, 24–7.

The 1–2–1 San Francisco 49ers are on the road to play the expansion 0–5 Atlanta Falcons for the first time. San Francisco gains 504 yards in total offense in the 44–7 victory. John Brodie completes a 10-yard touchdown pass to Pro Bowl wide receiver Dave Parks to start the scoring in the 1st quarter. Brodie completes 12 of 19 for 164 yards, and

John David Crow and Ken Willard combine to gain 88 yards rushing in the 1st half to stoke the 49er furnace.

Leading 24–7 in the 3rd quarter, future Hall of Fame corner Jimmy Johnson steals Dennis Claridge's pass and scoots 35 yards for a touchdown. Future Hall of Fame strong side linebacker Dave Wilcox leads a defense that allows just 59 yards rushing by Atlanta. Right defensive end Clark Miller of the 49ers is a thorn in the Falcon pass pocket all day, as San Francisco records 5 sacks.

Late in the 3rd quarter, Brodie tosses to running back Jimmy Jackson for 63 yards and a touchdown (the only TD of his career). Lee Calland of the Falcons blocks Tommy Davis's extra point attempt; this is just the second and final miss of Davis's outstanding career with the 49ers.

1977   The Seattle Seahawks are at home to face the winless Tampa Bay Buccaneers (0–18). Seahawk quarterback Steve Myer throws 4 touchdown passes (he throws only 6 in his career) to highlight the 30–23 victory. Future Hall of Fame receiver Steve Largent catches 2 touchdown passes in the 1st half, as Seattle leads 17–13. Leading 24–23 in the 4th quarter, Myer tosses to running back Sherman Smith for 44 yards (151 yards rushing and receiving in the game) and a touchdown to put the Seahawks ahead by 7. The Seahawk secondary intercepts 4 passes in securing the victory.

17

1937   Rookie Vern Huffman of the 3–1 Lions returns an errant Brooklyn Dodger pass 100 yards for a touchdown in the 3rd quarter to become the first player in league history to return an interception 100 yards. Detroit defeats

Brooklyn, 30–0. Huffman is the harbinger of outstanding Lion pass defenders over the next 40 years.

1943   Six years to the day and this time the 2–2 Lions are in Chicago to play the 0–3 Cardinals. Detroit ends up with minus yardage rushing (–53), while Chicago manages just 38 yards on 38 carries, thus the record for fewest yards gained rushing in a game by both teams with –15.

The Cardinals will continue to lose (0–10), as they throw 39 interceptions during the season and display the least efficient pass defense in the league (80.1). The only Lion score in the 7–0 victory is a 67–yard touchdown pass by Frank Sinkwich to Harry Hopp. The Lion pass defense is keyed by future Hall of Famer Alex Wojciechowicz, who records 1 of the 3 Detroit interceptions.

1954   Coach Jim Trimble takes his 3–0 contending Eagles on the road to battle the 0–3 Redskins. The Eagles allow only 514 yards rushing in their seven victories (73 yards a game), and today Washington gains just 28 yards on 20 carries against Philadelphia's front wall led by Pro Bowl linebackers Chuck Bednarik and Wayne Robinson and lineman Bucko Kilroy and Norm Willey.

Adrian Burk becomes just the second quarterback in league history to throw 7 touchdown passes in a game, as Philadelphia defeats the Redskins, 49–21. Later in the season, Burk throws 5 touchdown passes against the Skins in the rematch; thus he completes 36 of 55 for 577 yards and 12 touchdowns when he sees burgundy and gold (he earns his only Pro Bowl berth).

The Washington Redskin secondary goes on to rank as one of the most porous in league history, as their pass defense efficiency mark is 90.8, while the league average is 61.7.

1964 In their first 59 games, New York has had just four individual 100-yard rushing performances. Rookie Matt Snell gains 180 yards rushing to set a new team record in the 2–1–1 Jet 24–21 victory over the 2–3 Oilers. Snell, in the past two weeks, has gained 348 yards on 57 carries in back-to-back Jet wins.

18

1953 The 2–1 Rams are at Briggs Stadium to take on the 3–0 defending league champion Lions. Ram kick returner Woodley Lewis ties a record as he gains 294 yards on kick returns. Lewis returns 3 punts for 120 yards, including a 78-yard touchdown, and 5 kickoffs for 174 yards, including a 69-yard return in the 31–19 Ram victory.

1963 Fenway Park is the site of the 3–3 Patriots and the visiting 2–3 Broncos. Babe Parilli sets a team record with 358 yards passing (he completes 21 of 31) and 2 touchdowns in a 40–21 victory. Gino Cappelletti scores 21 points, and Larry Garron sets a league record for average yards per play as he gains 244 yards on 15 touches (16.26).

Fullback Billy Joe of Denver busts up the middle on a 68-yard touchdown run in the 2nd quarter to give the Broncos a short-lived 14–10 lead. Besides this run, the bruising Boston defense allows just 27 yards rushing on 17 carries and registers 7 sacks.

1964 The 2–3 49ers are in the Coliseum to air it out against the 2–2–1 Rams. Rookies Dave Parks of San Francisco (3 catches for 114 yards) and Bucky Pope of the Rams (4 catches for 141 yards, all in the 1st half) are the early focal point in this game. It is the first time in the history of this rivalry that a rookie for each team will gain more than 100 yards receiving in the same game.

Bucky "The Catawba Claw" Pope gains 786 yards receiving on just 25 catches for the season (6 of which are touchdown receptions of 48 yards or longer). Ram quarterback Roman Gabriel throws 4 touchdown passes (3 to Pope) in the 1st half (he completes 7 of 13 for 171 yards) as Los Angeles leads 28–7 (the 49er touchdown is by Parks on an 83-yard score) at the half. In the 2nd half, Gabriel completes just 1 of 9 passes for –1 yard, yet the Rams score twice due to their record-setting pass defense.

It is the 2nd quarter, and Aaron Martin returns an interception 36 yards, while Jerry Richardson returns an interception 35 yards. Then in the 3rd quarter, Richardson tallies 2 interception returns for 16 and 41 yards. And in the 4th quarter, Frank Budka turns in an 18-yard interception return, and finally Bobby Smith goes 97 yards for a touchdown and Martin 71 yards for a touchdown on interceptions. There are a total of 7 Los Angeles interceptions for a record-setting 314 yards in the 42–14 Ram victory.

19

1969 The 2–3 Broncos are at Nippert Stadium in Cincinnati to take on the 3–2 Bengals. The Broncos gain a season high 421 yards in total offense, including 272 rushing. In their first 118 games as a franchise, the Broncos had just five individual rushing performances of 100 yards. Floyd Little sets a team record (at this point in team history) with 166 yards rushing, his fifth in Denver's last 14 games.

Denver leads 16–6 in the 2nd quarter, when Little scoots 48 yards for a touchdown. Later in the quarter, Steve Tensi throws his 2nd touchdown pass of the game, as Denver leads 30–6 at the half. Cincinnati rallies behind Sam Wyche's two 2nd-half touchdown passes, yet Denver hangs on to win, 30–23. The key to the Denver defense is a record-setting pass rush, which registers 10 sacks, 4 of which are by all-AFL left defensive end Rich "Tombstone" Jackson, with 4.

1997   The 6–0 Denver Broncos are in Oakland to battle the 2–4 Raiders. Raider running back Napoleon Kaufman sets a team record as he gains 227 yards rushing on 28 carries in the 28–25 Oakland victory. Denver leads 17–14 late in the 3rd quarter, when Raider safety Eric Turner returns a fumble 65 yards for the go-ahead score. With seven minutes left in the game, Kaufman explodes for an 83-yard touchdown to clinch the victory. John Elway throws for 309 yards on 26 completions, including a late 28-yard touchdown pass to Ed McCaffrey, but the Broncos fall out of the saddle.

2003   The 0–5 Chargers are on the road in Cleveland to play the 3–3 Browns. For the third time in his short career, running back LaDainian Tomlinson gains at least 200 yards rushing in a game. San Diego leads 13–6 in the 3rd quarter, when Tomlinson sprints 70 yards for a touchdown. Although Kelly Holcomb of the Browns throws two 4th-quarter touchdown passes, it is not enough. The Chargers earn their first victory of the season, 26–20. Tomlinson goes on to finish third in the league in rushing, with 1,645 yards.

20

1963   The 4–1 Chargers journey to Municipal Stadium in Kansas City for the first time to take on the 2–2–1 Chiefs.

When Len Dawson completes a 73-yard touchdown pass to Abner Haynes (8 catches for 149 yards), the Chiefs lead 7–3 at the half.

San Diego comes roaring back in the 2nd half, as Tobin Rote (16 of 22 for 266 yards) finds Lance Alworth open for 44- and 73-yard touchdown passes. Alworth continues on to set a team record that lasts 19 years by gaining 232 yards receiving in a game.

Dawson (16 of 24 for 225 yards) completes a 7-yard touchdown pass to Fred Arbanas to cut the lead to 7 in the 4th quarter. Keith Lincoln bolts 76 yards for a touchdown to give San Diego an insurmountable lead as the Chargers go on to win 38–17. Lincoln is the only Charger in team history to average at least 12.7 yards per carry twice in a game (10 for 127).

1968 The 2–3 Denver Broncos are on the road in San Diego to play the 4–1 Chargers. San Diego sets a team record for total offense in a game with 581 yards (which lasts 17 years). Dickie Post gains 121 rushing, while Jacque MacKinnon, Gary Garrison, and Lance Alworth combine to gain 380 yards receiving on just 12 catches. Quarterback John Hadl completes 9 passes for 321 yards and 4 touchdowns as San Diego outscores Denver 55–24.

Defensive back Joe Beauchamp of the Chargers returns a Steve Tensi pass 35 yards for a touchdown in the 2nd quarter (Beauchamp will return his 10 interceptions against the Broncos 219 yards). Rookie Marlin Briscoe gains 305 yards in total offense (68 rushing and 237 passing) when he replaces an injured Tensi. San Diego has defeated Denver nine of their past ten games and averaged 37 points a game in those victories.

In Kansas City, the 5–1 Chiefs host the 4–1 Raiders in a highly competitive division race. Coach Hank Stram unleashes a full house backfield and ravages the defending AFL champion Raiders with 60 running plays (then a team record) for 294 yards, as Mike Garrett (109), Robert Holmes (95), and Wendell Hayes (89) control both the ball and clock in the 24–10 turnover-free showdown victory. The Chiefs set a league record by attempting just 3 passes in the game (Len Dawson completes 2).

21

1956 The 1–2 Rams are at Milwaukee County Stadium for their clash with the 1–2 Packers. Billy Howton breaks Don Hutson's team record for yardage receiving in a game with 257 yards (the third most in league history at that time). Tobin Rote finds Howton for a 36-yard touchdown in the 1st quarter to tie the game at 7. Howton catches 5 passes for 168 yards in the 2nd quarter, including a 63-yard halfback option pass from Jack Losch for a touchdown. Ahead 28–17 in the 4th quarter, Rote completes a 53-yard streak to Howton to set up his own 2-yard run to put the game out of reach.

1973 We have the same teams 17 years later but a different venue as we are in the Coliseum with the 2–1–2 defending NFC Central Division champion Packers clashing with the 5–0 Rams. Larry Smith of the Rams has scored from the 1-yard line with 11:33 left in the game to give Los Angeles a 20–7 lead. Green Bay has 1st down and 21 to go on their own 12, when right defensive end Fred Dryer sacks Scott Hunter in the end zone.

Right linebacker Fred Carr of the Packers recovers a

Ram fumble on his own 8-yard line with seven minutes left in the game. Green Bay has 1st and 10 on their own 22, when future Hall of Fame left defensive end Jack Young-blood sacks Jim Del Gaizo for an 11-yard loss, now 2nd and 21. Here he comes again, as Dryer sacks Del Gaizo in the end zone for his 2nd safety in the quarter. Dryer is the only player in league history to record 2 safeties in a game. Green Bay gains just 63 yards in total offense in the game. Los Angeles finishes leading the league in total defense, and in their 12 victories they allow just 203 yards a game.

1973 The 2–3 Saints travel to Candlestick Park to take on the 2–3 defending NFC Western Division champions. Future Hall of Fame left linebacker Dave Wilcox leads a defensive effort in which New Orleans gains just 82 yards in total offense (the best effort of the season by the 49ers). In his last seven games against the 49ers as a Saint, wide receiver Danny Abramowicz caught 30 passes for 576 yards. Now a 49er, Abramowicz catches 4 passes for 101 yards and his only touchdown of the season in a 40–0 win. Tom Wittum dashes 63 yards (the second-longest run ever against the Saints by a 49er) on a fake punt.

22

1961 The 4–1 49ers, with their spread formation ("shot-gun") offense, journey to Wrigley Field to take on the 3–2 Bears. Defensive coach Clark Shaughnessy, with able assistance from secondary coach George Allen, has a game plan to defuse the "shotgun" formation that has scored 167 points in five games thus far in the season. By aligning the defensive ends wider, arranging the outside linebackers inside on the offensive tackles, putting the middle linebacker

(Hall of Famer Bill George) up on the center, and deploying five defensive backs ("nickle") when John Brodie is substituted into the game, the Bears can attack the San Francisco offense.

Chicago quarterback Bill Wade throws 2 touchdown passes in the 1st half, as the Bears lead 14–0. San Francisco gains 85 yards rushing and 43 yards passing (4 of 8). In the 2nd half, the 49ers gain just 7 yards rushing on 12 attempts and complete just 1 pass out of 10 attempts (for –3 yards) as the Bear defense controls the game. Chicago takes the ball away from San Francisco 6 times to give their offense excellent field position. Rookie Mike Ditka enters the game with 15 catches for 337 yards, and in the game he continues his assault on secondaries as he catches 4 passes for 107 yards and 2 key touchdowns. The Chicago running game churns out 149 yards on 35 carries in the 31–0 victory.

1967   The 3–1–1 Jets travel to Miami to play the 1–4 Dolphins. Future Hall of Fame quarterbacks Joe Namath and Bob Griese hit the target on almost every pass. Namath completes 13 of 15 for 199 yards and 2 touchdowns. His main weapons, Don Maynard and George Sauer, combine to catch 10 passes for 190 yards (they go on to finish 1–2 in the AFL in receptions and yards for the season). Griese sets a team record that lasts 11 years by completing 81 percent of his passes (17 of 21). The Dolphin running game is limited to 78 yards on 22 attempts by the improving New York defense in the 33–14 Jet victory.

2000   The 4–3 Broncos are in Cincinnati to play the 0–6 Bengals. Cincinnati leads 17–14 entering the 4th quarter. Corey Dillon scores twice on touchdown runs of 65 and 41 yards, as he sets the Cincinnati team rushing record of 278 yards on 22 carries in the 31–21 victory.

23

1966 The 4–2 Chiefs are at Mile High Stadium to take on the 1–5 Broncos. Kansas City gains 614 total yards in offense, which is still the team record 42 years later. Running back Bert Coan gains 111 yards rushing and scores 4 of his career 19 touchdowns in this game, as Kansas City destroys Denver, 56–10. The Chiefs gain 380 yards rushing (the second most in a game in team history). The Chiefs continue on to average 188 yards a game rushing in their 11 victories on their way to the AFL title. Denver gains a season low 28 yards rushing (14 attempts), as the Chiefs defense averages giving up just 91 yards a game in their 11 wins. Kansas City safeties Bobby Hunt and Johnny Robinson, who tie for the interception title with 10 each, pick off 2 in this game.

1988 The 3–3–1 Jets are in Miami to face the 4–3 Dolphins and Dan Marino. There are 97 passes thrown in the game, and neither quarterback is sacked. What happens when the ball is in the air is what sets this game apart.

For the eighth time in his career, Marino throws for more than 400 yards (he holds the record with 13). He completes 35 of 60 for the second most passing yards in a game, with 521. Mark Clayton and Mark Duper of the Dolphins combine to catch 16 passes for 285 yards.

New York leads 13–10 in the 2nd quarter, when Erik McMillan pilfers a Marino pass and goes 55 yards for a touchdown (he intercepts 3). Down 30–10 at the half, Marino keeps firing and firing as Miami cuts the lead to

37–30. The Jets score late to win 44–30 as their 5 interceptions prove to be the difference.

1994 The 3–4 Rams are in New Orleans to take on the 2–5 Saints. It is the 2nd quarter, and the Rams are kicking off after cutting the Saint lead to 17–14. Tyrone Hughes returns the kick 92 yards for a touchdown. Hughes returns a Ram kickoff 98 yards for a touchdown to close the 3rd quarter and a 37–20 lead. Hughes sets records for most yards on kickoff returns in a game with 304 (breaking a 44-year-old record) and combined kick return yards with 347. Robert Bailey of the Rams returns a Saint punt a league record 103 yards for a touchdown late in the game as New Orleans hangs on to win, 37–34.

24

1948 Coach Jimmy Conzelman has the Cardinals headed in the right direction, as they have won 16 of their last 22 regular-season games. The Boston Yanks take an early 6–0 lead and have the ball in the 2nd quarter. Linebacker Bill Blackburn intercepts and returns the theft 31 yards for a touchdown. Leading 14–6 in the 3rd quarter, Blackburn returns his 2nd interception 27 yards for a touchdown to become the first Cardinal in team history to return 2 interceptions for a touchdown in the same game.

The Chicago offense is sparked by future Hall of Famer Charlie Trippi, who registers his first 100-yard rushing game, as he gains 104 yards on just 9 carries. This is only the eighth time in the last 15 years that a team has combined a player rushing for 100 yards and had a teammate return an interception for a touchdown (all resulting in victories). The Yanks score three 4th-quarter touchdowns, but it is too little too late in the 49–26 Chicago victory.

1965 The 2–3 Vikings are at Kezar Stadium to shoot it out with the 3–2 49ers. John Brodie enters the game having completed 97 of 140 (69.2 percent) for 1,190 yards (8.5 yards per pass) with 11 touchdowns. Brodie has another excellent day throwing the pigskin as he completes 19 of 29 for 264 yards against Minnesota with 3 going for touchdowns to flanker Bernie Casey. Fran Tarkenton is the best passer on the field, however, as he completes 21 of 34 for 407 yards (a new team record) and 3 touchdowns in the 42–41 come-from-behind win. Paul Flatley of the Vikings sets a team record as he gains 202 yards receiving on 7 receptions.

San Francisco builds a 35–14 3rd-quarter lead, but here comes the relentless Viking attack. When Tarkenton fires a 58-yard touchdown strike to Flatley in the 4th quarter, Minnesota leads for the first time, 42–38. San Francisco goes on to lead the league in total offense (376 yards a game) and scoring with 421 points during the season.

1976 The defending NFC champion Vikings have won 39 of their last 48 games and are at the Vet to play the Eagles. Chuck Foreman becomes the first Viking in history to gain 200 yards rushing (30 attempts) in a 31–12 victory over Philadelphia.

25

1964 The 0–5–1 Raiders host the 1–5 Broncos at Frank Youell Field. Clem Daniels gains 167 yards rushing (the third most in his career) to key the ground attack, while

AFL all-star quarterback Francis "Cotton" Davidson becomes the seventh passer in league history to throw for more than 400 yards (he completes 23 of 36 with 5 touchdowns). Art Powell and Billy Cannon combine to catch 16 passes for 255 yards and 4 touchdowns. The Raiders set a league record by gaining 626 yards in total offense in the 40–7 victory.

The 3–3 Vikings are at Kezar Stadium to battle the 2–4 49ers. San Francisco leads at the half 17–10 as John Brodie and George Mira complete 12 of 22 for 226 yards. Outstanding rookie wide receiver Dave Parks gains 124 yards on 3 catches (including an 80-yard touchdown in the 2nd quarter).

Fran Tarkenton's 8-yard dash gives the Vikings a 20–17 3rd-quarter lead. Mira fumbles when hit by Jim Marshall, and rookie left defensive end Carl Eller strides 45 yards for a touchdown with the fumble recovery. In the next series and on 1st and 20, Mira completes a pass to Billy Kilmer, who fumbles (stripped by Karl Kassulke). Right defensive end Marshall, attempting to duplicate the feat of his teammate, scoops up the ball and away he goes the wrong way to score a safety for San Francisco (60 yards). The Viking defense stays the course even with the gaffe and wins, 27–22.

1971 We have Monday night football at the Met, as the 4–1 defending Super Bowl champion Colts clash with the 4–1 defending NFC Central champion Vikings. Both teams have demonstrated successful zone pass defense through the first five weeks of the season.

Colt opponents have completed just 62 of 125 for 540 yards, and Viking opponents have completed just 72 of

145 for 738 yards. Two red zone interceptions stop Colt drives, and Ed "Bozo" Sharockman returns an Earl Morrall pass to the Baltimore 23 to set up the only touchdown of the game in a vicious 10–3 Viking victory.

Hard-hitting right corner Sharockman also spills Tom Matte on a 3rd and 1 sweep inside the 10 to keep the Colts out of the end zone. The Colts allow only 17 offensive touchdowns all season, while Minnesota allows only 12 as both teams return to the play-offs.

26

1947   The 1–2–1 Boston Yanks are at Comiskey Park to take on the 3–1 Cardinals. Chicago end Billy Dewell, who catches 9 passes for 116 yards and 2 touchdowns, leads the Cardinals to a 27–7 victory. For the second consecutive week, Boston halfback Frank Seno records an interception. Seno is the first player in league history (although it is not ever credited) to intercept in six consecutive games. Seno goes on to lead the league in punt return average (17.8) and interceptions with 10 (along with Frank Reagan).

1969   The 3–3 Cincinnati Bengals are in Kansas City to play the 5–1 Chiefs. The punishing Chief defense allows the Bengals just 65 yards rushing in a 42–22 victory. Kansas City continues on to limit opponents to only 77 yards a game rushing in their 11 victories during the season. The Kansas City offense, with Warren McVea gaining 141 yards rushing (including the Chiefs longest run of the year, 80 yards), totals 313 yards on the ground. Mike Garrett gains 101 yards receiving, and Mike Livingston throws 3 touchdown passes. The Chiefs pass rush is on the warpath today as well, with 6 sacks.

1980 The 2–5 St. Louis Cardinals are on the road in Baltimore to battle the 4–3 Colts. The Cardinals build a 17–0 3rd-quarter lead, as wide receiver Mel Gray gains 101 yards receiving on 7 catches to pace the offense. Rookie defensive lineman Curtis Greer registers 4½ sacks as he leads the attack on the Colt pass pocket that produces a team record 12 sacks.

We are in the Astrodome in Houston to witness Earl Campbell gain more than 200 yards rushing (202 on 27 carries) for the second consecutive week. In the 3rd quarter, Campbell bolts through the Bengal defense on his longest run of the season (55 yards) for the go-ahead touchdown. He also scores in the 4th quarter as the 4–3 Oilers go on to defeat the 3–4 Bengals 20–3. Campbell gains the second-most yards rushing in a season with 1,934 and is the first runner to ever record four 200-yard rushing games in a season.

27

1957 The 1–3 Eagles are in Pittsburgh to battle the 2–2 Steelers under new coach Buddy Parker. Unusual for Parker, he has 15 rookies on his squad as well as a young quarterback that he has traded for, Earl Morrall. For just the second time in their last 89 games, the Steelers pitch a shutout as they defeat Philadelphia, 6–0. Morrall (who earns a Pro Bowl berth in his only full season in Pittsburgh) finds Ray Mathews for 35 yards and a touchdown in the 2nd quarter for the only score.

The stalwart Steeler defense, led by Pro Bowl middle linebacker Dale Dodrill and future Hall of Fame right defensive tackle Ernie Stautner, limits the Eagles to just 70 yards rushing (31 attempts). They also lead a pass rush that sacks Eagle quarterbacks 3 times for 31 yards.

Rookie Sonny Jurgensen, fresh off a 6 of 9 passing performance in an upset of Cleveland, is pressured into a 1 of 5 passing performance for just 12 yards. He is intercepted by league interception champion Jack Butler (who has 10 for the season). The rest of the Eagle passers gain 19 yards on 3 of 8 passing, so for the game Philadelphia gains 0 net yards passing.

1968   The 2–5 Bengals are in Oakland to play the defending AFL champion Raiders. For the third consecutive week, the 11 angry men who comprise the Raider defense allow a 100-yard rusher (they allowed none in their 1967 championship season). Paul Robinson of Cincinnati records the first 100-yard rushing performance in franchise history, as he gains 159 yards on 17 carries. His performance is a team record for 11 years. On the other 37 Bengal offensive plays, they gain 69 yards total.

In the 2nd quarter, Robinson breaks free for an 87-yard touchdown jaunt to cut the lead in half, 14–7. The silver and black continue to pound away at the expansion defense and gain a season high 265 yards rushing. Warren Wells catches 5 passes for 118 yards to key the pass offense. The Raiders have rebounded from their tough loss to Kansas City to improve to 5–2 in their race for the AFL Western crown.

1996   The winless Jets (0–8) travel to the desert and defeat the 3–4 Cardinals, as Adrian Murrell sets a team record with 199 yards rushing on 31 attempts. Leading 17–14 early in the 4th quarter, Murrell gives New York a 10-point lead on a 1-yard run as the Jets prevail 31–21.

28

1934 The Portsmouth Spartans have moved to Detroit, yet today we are back at Universal Stadium in Portsmouth to watch the first-place 6–0 Lions play the Cincinnati Reds. Future Hall of Famer Earl "Dutch" Clark gains a team record 194 yards rushing on 24 carries, including an 82-yard touchdown run in the 3rd quarter. Clark also dropkicks a 1st-quarter field goal in the 38–0 victory. For seven consecutive weeks, the Lions rock-ribbed defense will shut out the opposition as all-pro's Ox Emerson, George Christensen, Bill McKalip, and Earl Clark are impregnable.

1956 Twenty-two years later and the Lions are again undefeated (4–0) in first place. Future Hall of Fame safety Yale Lary is the difference maker in this game. Norm Van Brocklin punts on 4th and 5 at his own 37, and Lary returns the ball 38 yards up the left sideline to the Ram 42. When the Detroit drive stalls, Bobby Layne kicks an 11-yard field goal. After another Lary punt return (12 yards), Layne drives the Lions 57 yards and kicks a 15-yard field goal.

Just before the half, Ram quarterback Billy Wade fires deep, and Lary intercepts on his own 3-yard line. Now in the 2nd half, Van Brocklin fires down the field, and Lary again intercepts (the pass was intended for Tom Fears). Layne directs a 76-yard drive, which he caps on a short run.

It is the 4th quarter, and Van Brocklin completes to Elroy Hirsch for 37 yards and a touchdown as the defending conference champions close the gap to 13–7. Detroit has 4th and 5 on their own 49, and Lary fakes the punt, twists away, and dashes up the left sideline for 10 yards and a 1st down. Jim Martin of the Lions kicks a 43-yard field goal. Late in the game, Van Brocklin is intercepted again by Lary (he is the original "Mr. October," as all 10 of his interceptions against the Rams come in this month), who weaves his way 31 yards to wrap up the 16–7 win.

1962 The first-place 4–0–2 Redskins are in Yankee Stadium to play the 4–2 Giants. Future Hall of Fame quarterback Y. A. Tittle becomes just the third man to throw 7 touchdown passes and the second quarterback to pass for more than 500 yards in a game. All-pro Del Shofner becomes the fifth receiver to gain more than 250 yards in a game (13 catches for 269 yards). Leading 21–20 in the 3rd quarter, Tittle fires 4 touchdown passes in the 2nd half as New York prevails, 49–34.

29

1950 The 4–2 Browns meet the 2–4 Steelers for their first-ever meeting at Municipal Stadium in Cleveland. Through the first six weeks, 30-year-old Marion Motley has gained only 233 yards rushing (he does not rank in the top ten) on 57 carries; however, today the future Hall of Famer sets a league record that still stands 58 years later as he averages 17.1 yards per carry. His 188 yards on 11 carries include a 69-yard touchdown run in the 3rd quarter in the 45–7 victory. Over the course of the last six games of the season (all victories), Motley gains 577 yards on just 83 carries (6.95 a carry) to win the rushing title. The opportunistic Cleveland defense intercepts 6 passes to help the cause.

In the West, the 4–2 Los Angeles Rams, like the Cleveland Browns, need to win to stay in the play-off race. In the Coliseum, the Lions are fed to the Rams 65–24 (they have now scored 245 points in five wins). Lions starting right half-back Wally Triplett begins the game with a 74-yard kickoff return that leads to a field goal. Triplett returns kickoffs for 81 and 97 yards in the 2nd quarter. Detroit trails 31–10 in the 3rd quarter, when Triplett makes his final kick return of 42 yards. Triplett still holds the record for kickoff return average for a game with 73.50 (294 on 4 returns). His yardage total remained the record for 44 years. Wally also gains 37 yards rushing on 6 carries in the 1st half. The prolific pass offense of the Rams gains 427 yards on 20 completions, including 5 Norm Van Brocklin touchdown passes.

1961   For the first time in pro football history, two future Hall of Fame quarterbacks throw for more than 400 yards on the same day. George Blanda completes 18 of 32 for 464 yards and 4 touchdowns (1 in each quarter). Charlie Hennigan (232 yards on 9 catches) and Bill Groman (100 yards on 2 catches) both score twice as the 2–3–1 Oilers defeat the 3–4 Bills 28–16.

Sonny Jurgensen completes 27 of 41 for 436 yards in a come-from-behind 27–24 victory over the winless Redskins. Pete Retzlaff and Tommy McDonald combine for 266 yards on 14 receptions and all 3 Philadelphia touchdowns. McDonalds's winning score comes with less than a minute remaining on a perfectly thrown post route. Blanda (as a Raider) and Jurgensen (as a Redskin) meet just once (1970).

30

1955   The 2–3 Bears are in the Coliseum to battle the first-place 4–1 Rams. Los Angeles safety Don Burroughs intercepts Ed Brown's 1st pass, and the Rams score first. In the 2nd quarter, George Blanda kicks a 48-yard field goal to give Chicago a 10–7 lead, yet what is remembered from this play is the photo of Burroughs standing in Eugene "Big Daddy" Lipscomb's cupped hands attempting to block the kick.

Blanda, now at quarterback, takes Chicago on an 81-yard drive as he completes all 6 of his passes (Hill scores on a 5-yard reception from Blanda). Chicago leads 17–7 at the half. After a Ron Waller touchdown run by the Rams, Brown returns and throws a beautiful 86-yard bomb to league MVP Harlon Hill to extend the Bear lead to 24–13. Hill scores his 3rd touchdown of the game (he catches 8 passes for 151 yards) on a 5-yard option pass from rookie Pro Bowl fullback Rick Casares, as the Bears go on to win, 31–20. The Ram defense allows more than 400 yards in total offense just twice all season (both to the Bears in losses), yet manages to hold off Chicago to win the division title in Sid Gillman's first year as coach.

1966   The 4–3 Raiders travel to Fenway Park in Boston to battle the 3–2–1 Patriots. In their first six years (84 games), the Patriots have had just seven individual 100-yard rushing performances. This season, however, is different as battering ram fullback Jim Nance rewrites the record book. Nance gains 208 yards rushing in this game (a team record that lasts 17 years) on 38 carries (an AFL league record) and 2 touchdowns in the 24–21 win.

Nance will gain more than 100 yards eight times during the season (again a league record), and Boston's record is 7–0–1 when he does. "By Land" is the Patriot motto for 1966, as they average 169 yards a game rushing when they win and only 102 when they do not. Nance goes on to set the league record with 1,458 yards rushing for the contending Patriots.

2005 The Giants not only dedicate the game to Wellington "The Duke" Mara, but shut out the Redskins for the first time in 44 years (36–0) in a battle for first place. Tiki Barber gains 206 yards rushing (he is the only Giant to gain more than 200 against Washington in team history) and sets a season record of 1,860 yards rushing.

31

1948 For the first time in league history, two quarterbacks will throw for more than 400 yards on the same day (and are only the second and third men to accomplish this impressive feat). So let us start our day with Sammy Baugh (now in the T formation) throwing for 446 yards on just 17 completions in the 59–21 victory over the green and gold Boston Yanks. Halfbacks Dick Todd and Tom Farmer combine to catch 10 passes for 261 yards as Washington gains 625 yards in total offense.

Rookie defensive halfback Dan Sandifer intercepts in his second consecutive game (he goes on to tie Frank Seno's league record of intercepting in six straight games and is never credited for his accomplishment). Not only does Sandifer intercept, but he returns a Yank pass 35 yards for a touchdown in the 1st quarter and 50 yards for a touchdown in the 4th quarter (again tying a league record). Sandifer (he and teammate Baugh are the only two men at this point in league history to intercept 4 passes in a game) also sets league records for interceptions in a season with 13 and yards returned with 254.

In the West at the Coliseum, Jim Hardy throws for 406 yards on 28 completions in a 27–22 loss to the defending league champion Cardinals.

1954 The 2–3 Bears are at Kezar Stadium to battle the 4–0–1 49ers. Rookie Harlon Hill sets a team record with 214 yards receiving (a record that still stands) and 4 crucial touchdowns in a 31–27 victory. Hill has recorded four 100-yard receiving games in the first six games of his career.

1966 The 5–1–1 first-place Cardinals are hosting the 3–3 Bears in a Monday night contest. Larry Wilson intercepts 3 passes, including a 29-yard 4th-quarter touchdown return in a 24–17 victory. Wilson's final interception of a deep "post pattern" to Dick Gordon sews up the win. He has now intercepted in six consecutive games and goes on to lead the league with 10.

1988 The 3–5 Colts host the 4–4 defending conference champion Broncos. Eric Dickerson gains 124 yards rushing in the 1st half (159 for the game) and scores 4 touchdowns in the game in a 55–23 victory (the most points ever scored on a Monday night).

November

1

1942 The Packers trail the undefeated Bears by one game and must win at home over the Cardinals to keep pace with Chicago. Although Cecil Isbell does not throw a pass until the 2nd quarter and his first 3 attempts are incomplete, he sets the league record by passing for 336 yards and averages 15.8 yards per pass. He completes only 10 of 21, yet 5 of his passes gain 276 yards, all for touchdowns. This also ties a league record.

For the first time in league history, teammates catch passes for more than 100 yards in a game. Don Hutson catches 5 for 207 yards, and Andy Uram catches 4 for 174 yards. Uram gains 162 yards receiving in the 2nd half, which is still the team record for yards receiving in a half 66 years later.

How good was Isbell? The records he set in this game are broken by Hall of Famers Sid Luckman and Sammy Baugh. Isbell also held the record for most consecutive games throwing a touchdown pass until John Unitas broke it.

1953 The talented San Francisco 49ers are 3–2 and trail the defending league champion Lions in the standings. They must win at Kezar Stadium against the Bears. More passes are attempted in this game than in any other in league history at this point in time (94).

Future Hall of Famers Y. A. Tittle of the 49ers and George Blanda of the Bears square off in this passing duel. Tittle completes 25 of 43 for 304 yards, and Blanda completes 29 of 46 for 233 yards. Just before the half, future Hall of Fame running back Hugh "The King" McElhenny scores on an 8-yard run to put San Francisco ahead, 21–14. Amazingly, with all the passes thrown, there are no touchdowns in the 2nd half as the 49ers win, 24–14.

2

1952 The 2–3 defending league champion Los Angeles Rams are hosting the woeful Dallas Texans in the Coliseum. League ground gaining champion "Deacon" Dan Towler paces the Ram offense with 111 yards rushing, including his longest run of the season, a 44-yard touchdown burst in the 1st quarter to get the Rams on the board.

The highest scoring team in the league rings up 42 points to take a commanding lead. This is the second of eight consecutive Ram victories that will again put them in the play-offs. During the 1952 season, the Ram defense goes on to score an unprecedented 8 touchdowns, including Herb Rich's 97-yard excursion down the right sideline with a Texan pass in the 2nd quarter. The game marks the first time in team history that a Ram will rush for more than 100 yards and have a teammate return an interception for a touchdown. The Rams have accomplished this feat more than any team in league history with 34.

Defensively, the Rams continue on to lead the league in pass defense efficiency, with a mark of 42.5. Rookie right corner Dick "Night Train" Lane and right safety Herb Rich set a record that still exists today, as they combine to intercept 22 passes on the season.

The Texans score 20 unanswered points in the 2nd half, including offensive tackle Gino Marchetti's only offensive touchdown on a 17-yard pass from Hank Lauricella. The Texans return Ram passes 182 yards to set a league record; the last interception return is a 66-yard touchdown return by former Cardinal Jerry Davis.

1997   The 1–7 Bengals are at home in Riverfront Stadium hosting the 4–4 Chargers. Eric Metcalf returns 4 punts for 168 yards, including touchdowns of 85 and 67 yards. Four of his 8 lifetime punt return touchdowns have come against Cincinnati. Eric Metcalf joins Hall of Famer Jack Christiansen as the only men to return 2 punts for a touchdown twice in a game. Metcalf eventually sets the standard, as he returns 10 punts for a touchdown in his career. Cincinnati wins the game, though, 38–31 behind Corey Dillon's punishing runs (he gains a total of 123 yards).

3

1968   The 3–4 Vikings are at home in the Metrodome against the Redskins. Minnesota builds a 20–0 halftime lead with a punishing defense (Washington gains only 41 yards rushing on 21 attempts). Free safety Paul Krause is in the midst of a six-game interception streak (he is the only player in league history to have two streaks of six or more). Rookie Charlie West returns a Washington 3rd-quarter punt 98 yards for a touchdown to tie the league record.

Minnesota continues to win and earns their first division title in team history.

Cleveland is 4–3 and on the road at Kezar Stadium in San Francisco. Defending league rushing champion Leroy Kelly has the biggest rushing performance of his career with 174 yards in the 33–21 victory. Kelly defends his rushing title, and the Browns return to the play-offs.

While at Lambeau Field in Green Bay, Gale Sayers establishes a new Bear record with 205 yards rushing in a 13–10 Chicago victory. The Bears are now 4–4 and tied with Minnesota for first place. Chicago wins the game on the rarely used "free kick," as Mac Percival drills home the winner from 43 yards as the Packers helplessly watch. Although Sayers loses the rushing title to Kelly, he earns the comeback player of the year award in 1969, as he wins the rushing title. All four rushing titles were won by either Kelly or Sayers from 1966 through 1969.

1985 Seventeen years to the day, another Bear, Walter Payton, provides the offense as he rushes for 192 yards on 28 carries and scores the winning touchdown on a 27-yard dash in the 4th quarter as Chicago prevails 16–10. William Perry scores the other Chicago touchdown on the only touchdown reception of his career. The Bears go on to win the Super Bowl.

1991 In RFK Stadium the Redskins remain undefeated as they defeat the Houston Oilers in overtime, 16–13. The "Hogs" remain the dominant force in Washington, as they have now allowed only 4 sacks in nine games. Ernest Byner keys the ground attack with 112 yards rushing. Joe Gibbs's best team goes on to win the Super Bowl.

4

1923 The 2–2–1 Packers must win to keep pace with the Canton Bulldogs and Chicago Bears to win the league title. On the road, Green Bay defeats the St. Louis All-Stars 3–0 in the mud at Sportsman's Park. Packer lineman Howard "Cub" Buck establishes a league record with 19 punts. The results of the Packers fourteen 1st-half possessions include 11 punts by Buck, a missed field goal attempt by Buck, and 2 Packer turnovers.

Late in the 3rd quarter, Buck's 50–yard punt is fumbled by Eber Simpson of St. Louis, and the Packers recover. Buck kicks a 20-yard field goal after 2 short running plays for the only points of the game. On the next Packer possession, a Buck quick kick on 1st down of 60 yards pins St. Louis inside their 10-yard line. Although Green Bay turns the ball over twice to St. Louis in the 4th quarter, Buck continues his superb punting to keep St. Louis deep into their own territory.

1945 At home in Griffith Stadium, the 3–1 Redskins host the Cardinals (who are wearing blue jerseys). Future Hall of Famer Sammy Baugh completes 19 of 25 for 229 yards. When the Cardinals rally in the 4th quarter to tie the game at 21, Baugh directs the Skins to the winning field goal.

1962 Charley Johnson completes 26 of 41 passing for a team record 365 yards in a 31–28 loss to the Giants in Yankee Stadium. Sonny Randle's 55-yard touchdown gives St. Louis a 21–17 3rd-quarter lead (Randle gains 256 receiving in the game on the second most catches ever in a game with 16). Y. A. Tittle throws his 3rd touchdown pass of the game in the 4th quarter in the victory.

Ernie Stautner registers a record-tying 3rd safety in the 3rd quarter of a 39–31 victory over the Vikings, as Pittsburgh improves to 4–4. Stautner goes on to recover 20 opponents' fumbles to rank second in league history in that category.

1984 The Seahawks return their 6 interceptions a league record 325 yards and for a record 4 touchdowns (Dave Brown, 2; Keith Simpson, 1; and Kenny Easley, 1) in crushing the Chiefs, 45–0.

5

1950 Green Bay, with a record of 2–4, travels to Baltimore to take on the winless Colts. The Colts gain more than 500 yards in total offense and win their only game of the year, 41–21. The Packers lead 21–14 entering the 4th quarter. Colt fullback Jim Spavital, in his only year in the NFL, has already scored twice on a 46-yard run and a 45-yard pass reception from quarterback Y. A. Tittle. Spavital gains 176 yards rushing on 15 carries (the rest of season he gains just 70 yards on 43 carries), including a 96-yard run to open the Colts 4th-quarter scoring.

Defensively, the Colts respond by returning 3 interceptions for a touchdown. Defensive end Jim Owens (in his only year in the NFL) scores from 25 yards out, halfback Frank Spaniel dashes 29 yards (in his only year in the NFL), and halfback Herb Rich weaves his way 45 yards for the final touchdown of the game. Rich goes on to have success with both the Los Angeles Rams and New York Giants.

The Colts are the first team in league history to return 3 interceptions for a touchdown in the same game. In addition, more interceptions have been returned for a touchdown on November 5 than any other date in pro football history.

1989   The 5–3 Rams are meeting the 5–3 Vikings in the Metrodome. Minnesota has 6 scoring drives end with Rich Karlis field goals. The Rams still lead 21–18 with eight seconds left, but Karlis again splits the uprights for a record-tying 7th field goal to put the game into overtime. Linebacker Mike Merriweather of Minnesota blocks Dale Hatcher's punt out of the back of the end zone for the winning safety. It is the first time since overtime was instituted in 1974 that a game ends on a safety.

The Vikings go on to win the NFC Central Division title and lose to the eventual Super Bowl champion 49ers in the divisional round of the play-offs. The Rams rebound from the Viking loss and win six of eight games down the stretch to earn a wild card berth. Los Angeles also loses to San Francisco in the play-offs.

6

1934   Tuesday football? At Temple Stadium, the 1–5 Philadelphia Eagles, who had scored just 7 points in their previous four games (all losses) explode against the winless Cincinnati Reds, 64–0, their last game before being disbanded. The point total is a new league record. Tailback Swede Hanson returns an interception for a touchdown and scores twice on the ground. Reds Weiner and Ed Matesic throw touchdown passes to right end Joe Carter (who ties the league record with 3 TD catches).

1955   George Halas claims that this will be his last year as head coach. After a 0–3 start, the Bears have won three straight and are in Wrigley Field to play their traditional rivals, the Packers, who are also 3–3. The Bears gain a season high 504 yards total offense, of which 406 yards are gained rushing (on 54 attempts). Rookie teammates Rick Casares and Bobby Watkins both gain more than 100 yards rushing (the first time in team history). This is the first time in league history that rookie teammates gain more than 100 yards rushing.

When Bill McColl scores on Chicago's 1st drive of the 4th quarter, the Bears are safely ahead 45–3, right? The navy blue and gold Packers respond by scoring 28 points in the quarter. Green Bay gains 234 yards on offense in the quarter (99 rushing and 135 passing) yet totals only 319 for the entire game. Pro Bowl fullback Howie Ferguson scores twice, and Tobin Rote completes 6 of 12 passing to provide the offense.

The comeback cannot be complete without the defense taking the ball away from Chicago, and to the rescue we have right safety Bobby Dan Dillon, who records two 4th-quarter interceptions (a 61-yard return sets up a 2nd Packer 4th-quarter touchdown). Dillon is the all-time nemesis in Bear history, with 11 interceptions for 301 yards (he is the only player in league history to return interceptions more than 300 yards against an opponent). The 42 points scored in the 4th quarter tie the league record. The 52 points scored by the Bears are the most scored in the rivalry up to this time.

1966 Although Philadelphia gains just 80 yards in total offense, the play-off bowl-bound Eagles win 24–23, as Timmy Brown is the first player in league history to return 2 kickoffs for a touchdown in a game.

7

1948 The 4–1–1 first-place Eagles visit the Polo Grounds to take on the 1–5 Giants. Philadelphia, the defending division champions, punish New York, 35–14. Tommy Thompson throws two 1st-half touchdown passes to future Hall of Famer Pete Pihos (5 catches for 125 yards). Thompson goes on to lead the league in touchdown passes with 25 while finishing with a passer rating of 98.4. The Eagle ground game takes over in the 2nd half as future Hall of Famer Steve Van Buren scores twice as he gains 143 yards rushing on 25 carries. Philadelphia halfback Bosh Pritchard contributes the Eagles longest run from scrimmage for the season with a 65-yard burst for a touchdown in the 3rd quarter.

During a five-game streak during the season (October 31–November 28), the Eagles gain a whopping 2,208 yards on offense (441 a game). Philadelphia closes out the season by winning their first title in a championship game rematch with the Chicago Cardinals.

1976 The 7–1 defending AFC East champion Baltimore Colts journey west to San Diego to take on the 4–4 Chargers. Baltimore wins their sixth straight game as Bert Jones completes 18 of 25 for 275 yards and 3 touchdowns. Providing a large measure of the 481 total Colt yards is Pro Bowl running back Lydell Mitchell, who has a season-high 216 yards from scrimmage (91 rushing and 125 receiving). Mitchell's receiving out of the backfield has been a focal point of the Colt attack during the season, as 57 of his 60 receptions came in victory.

Although Jones finishes second to Ken "Snake" Stabler in the passer rating department (102.5), his consistency throughout the season was impressive. He completed 171 of 264 for 2,487 yards with 22 touchdowns and only 6 interceptions in the 11 Colt victories, yet he threw for more than 300 yards just once. Baltimore goes on to win the AFC East again.

8

1970   The 1–5–1 New Orleans Saints are at home in Tulane Stadium against Detroit. Future Hall of Famer Charlie Sanders's touchdown reception in the 3rd quarter puts the Lions ahead, 14–6. Short pass completions by Billy Kilmer to Dan Abramowicz (the defending league receiving champion) are the key components of the Saints offense in the game. New Orleans positions Tom Dempsey to attempt his 4th field goal of the game—a 63 yarder—and it is good. It is the second and last Saint victory of the season, while the Lions rebound and earn the first wild card berth in league history.

1987   The 4–3 Buccaneers travel to Busch Stadium to take on the 2–5 Cardinals in their final year in St. Louis. Tampa Bay builds a 28–3 lead early in the 4th quarter. The Cardinals launch the greatest 4th-quarter comeback in league history behind the effective passing of Neil Lomax and a suddenly suffocating defense. Lomax completes 25 of 36 for 314 yards (he is 10 of 13 in the 4th quarter for 164 yards and 3 touchdowns). J. T. Smith and rookie Robert Awalt combine for 17 catches for 220 yards, including the 3 Lomax tosses for 3 touchdowns. The Bucs drive 59 yards late in the 4th quarter, but Donald Igwebuike's 53-yard field goal attempt hits the crossbar as the Cardinals prevail 31–28. Tampa Bay does not win another game during the season, while St. Louis pockets five of their final eight games.

1992 The resurgent Steelers are 6–2 and on the road to take on the first-place 6–2 Buffalo Bills in Orchard Park. Thurman Thomas provides the Bills league-leading rushing attack with 155 yards on 37 carries. Thomas's 3rd-quarter touchdown run puts Buffalo ahead, 21–3, and the Bills hang on to win, 28–20. Buffalo continues to win and becomes just the second team in the AFC since the merger to advance to the Super Bowl for three consecutive years. Pittsburgh goes on to host and lose the rematch to Buffalo in the divisional round of the play-offs.

9

1941 The 2–6 Cleveland Rams are at Wrigley Field to take on the defending league champion 5–1 Chicago Bears. The league-leading Bear ground attack gains 245 yards rushing on 57 carries. Although there are many talented runners on the Bears roster, one man stands out. Future Hall of Famer George McAfee gains 65 yards rushing on just 7 carries and at this point in the season is averaging 8.4 yards per carry. McAfee goes on to lead the league in this category.

McAfee continues on to set a new league record for touchdowns scored in a season with 12 (Don Hutson also scores 12). Chicago leads 25–13 in the 4th quarter, when linebacker Bill Osmanski of the Bears intercepts and returns 19 yards before he laterals to McAfee. McAfee proceeds to weave, twist, and cut back 41 yards for the final touchdown. McAfee has never been credited for the additional interception return yards. Chicago goes on to defend their title, as McAfee stars in both play-off games against the Packers and Giants.

1958 The 4–2 Giants are at home in Yankee Stadium against the undefeated 6–0 Baltimore Colts. Although the Vince Lombardi–led New York offense gains 341 yards and has a 24–21 4th-quarter lead, the key to the game is the Giant pass defense. Future Hall of Famer Lenny Moore catches 6 passes for 181 yards and causes Giants defensive coordinator Tom Landry to rethink his defensive strategy for the December rematch. The Giants hang on to win, as future Hall of Famer Sam Huff makes a crucial interception of a George Shaw pass to halt the last Colt drive.

1980 The 6–3 Atlanta Falcons are in St. Louis to play the 3–6 Cardinals. The Jim Hart–led Cardinals have built a 27–13 4th-quarter lead. Pro Bowl running back William Andrews gains 115 yards rushing, and Pro Bowl quarterback Steve Bartkowski passes for 378 yards to lead the Falcons and the comeback. Atlanta wins in overtime, 33–27, and goes on to win their first division title in team history.

10

1963 The 7–1 Chargers travel to Boston to take on the 5–4 Patriots. Both teams are in the race for their respective division titles. Veteran quarterback Tobin Rote (one of just three men in pro football history to earn a Pro Bowl berth in both the NFL and AFL All-Star Games) tosses a 27-yard touchdown pass to Lance Alworth in the 1st quarter. That is all the Chargers need in holding off Boston, 7–6.

Alworth catches 13 passes for 210 yards in the game as San Diego gains just 271 total yards on the day. During a

58-game stretch in this future Hall of Famer's career, Alworth catches 301 passes for 6,189 yards (averaging 106 yards per game) and 57 touchdowns. The Patriots travel to Balboa Stadium at the end of the season to seek revenge in the AFL Championship Game.

1974 The 5–3 Cincinnati Bengals host the first-place 6–1–1 Pittsburgh Steelers at Riverfront Stadium. Ken Anderson sets an NFL record for highest completion percentage in a game as he completes 20 of 22 for 227 yards. Anderson's ability to keep drives alive with his accurate passing against the cover-two Steeler defense allows the Bengals to build a 17–10 4th-quarter lead. When safety Mike Wagner of Pittsburgh scoops up a Bengal fumble inside his own 10, he sets sail on a 65-yard fumble return only to be knocked out of bounds by Anderson on a game-saving tackle.

All-pro wide receiver Isaac Curtis, after a tremendous performance the week before against the Colts, is held to just 1 reception for 5 yards. Running back Doug Dressler catches 9 passes out of the backfield for 84 yards. Charlie Joiner and Chip Myers combine to catch 5 passes for 82 yards.

Ken Anderson goes on to win the passing title with a rating of 95.7, while the Steelers lead the league in the defensive passer rating system with a mark of 44.3. Pittsburgh rebounds from this loss and goes on to win their first of six Super Bowl titles.

11

1962 The last time the Eagles hosted the Packers at Franklin Field, they won the NFL title. Since that loss

Green Bay is 19–3, while Philadelphia so far in 1962 has won just one of eight games. Green Bay sets team records for 1st downs in a game with 37 and yards gained with 628. The productive receiving duo of Max McGee and Boyd Dowler catch 14 passes for 275 yards, while future Hall of Famer and 1962 league rushing champion Jim Taylor gains 141 yards on 25 carries. Taylor scores 2 touchdowns rushing in both the 2nd and 3rd quarter as Green Bay takes a commanding 49–0 lead by the end of the 3rd quarter.

The Packer defense does their part, as the Eagles gain just 54 yards in total offense. Hall of Fame quarterback Sonny Jurgensen completes just 4 of 13 passes for 35 yards. Green Bay's front seven limit the Eagles to 30 yards rushing on 13 carries and records 4 sacks. The Packers continue on to win their second consecutive league title.

1990   The 3–5 Seattle Seahawks travel to Arrowhead Stadium to play the 5–3 Kansas City Chiefs. Seattle quarterback Dave Krieg passes for 306 yards in the game, but the Seahawks trail late in the 4th quarter, 16–10. Outside linebacker Derrick Thomas has made life miserable for Krieg, as he sets the official league record for sacks in a game with 7. Krieg evades Thomas's attempt at sack number 8 and throws down the middle of the field to Paul Skansi for 25 yards and the winning touchdown. The Chiefs recover from the loss and return to the play-offs for the first time in four years.

2001   The 6–1 first-place Raiders head to Seattle to play the 3–4 Seahawks. Rich Gannon's accurate short passing helps Oakland gain a 20–13 lead in the 3rd quarter. Running back Shaun Alexander of Seattle sets a team record with 266 yards rushing on 35 carries, including an 88-yard touchdown run in the 3rd quarter to give the Seahawks a lead they never relinquish. The Raiders recover from the loss and go on to win the AFC Western Division title.

12

1961 The Chargers have won 13 consecutive regular-season games and are traveling to Bears Field in Denver to take on the 36 Broncos. The Bronco defense dominates the 1st half, and Denver leads 9–0. Jack Kemp's 91-yard touchdown pass to rookie Keith Lincoln (the longest pass play in the Chargers first 34 years) puts San Diego on the board in the 3rd quarter.

The Charger secondary, coached by Chuck Noll, goes on to set records that still exist today. When free agent all-league right corner Dickie Harris returns a Bronco-misfired pass 30 yards for a touchdown, he becomes the first player in pro football history to return 3 interceptions for a touchdown in a season. Harris's return gives the Chargers a 12–9 lead, and they go on to win 19–16.

San Diego still holds the record for most interceptions as a team (49) and touchdown returns (9) for a season. The Chargers return to the AFL Championship Game against the Houston Oilers.

1967 Baltimore, at 6–0–2, is in a desperate fight with the Rams for the Coastal Division title and cannot afford to lose. Atlanta, with a record of 1–6–1, is hosting the Colts and proceeds to get bombed by one John Unitas. Unitas gains 370 yards on just 20 passes (18.50), the second best average per pass in league history (behind Sammy Baugh) in the 49–7 Colt victory.

In the two games against the Falcons in 1967, Unitas completes 39 of 52 for 771 yards and 6 touchdowns. The Colts do not lose a game the first 13 weeks of the season in hopefully setting up a showdown with Central Division champion Green Bay, who is in Cleveland to play the first-place (Century Division) Browns. Green Bay keeps their hold on first place with an explosive 55–7 victory. The Packers and Browns combine for a record-setting 42 points in the 1st quarter. Rookie Travis Williams returns 2 kick-offs for a touchdown in the 1st half (tying a league record). The Packers gain 456 yards in total offense and record 7 takeaways on defense. Green Bay continues on to return to the Super Bowl and a date with destiny.

13

1955   The Lions have won the division title the past three years but enter this game at Forbes Field in Pittsburgh with a record of 1–6. The Steelers, at 4–3, still have designs on a division title but fall behind early and are forced to pass, and pass they do as Jim Finks and Ted Marchibroda complete 28 of 47 for 367 yards.

Starting at right corner for Detroit is second-year man Bill Stits (he earned a Pro Bowl berth the year before), and he now is in the rotation in the offensive backfield. With a 17–7 lead in the 3rd quarter, Stits begins a sweep left, pulls up, and throws an option pass 21 yards to future Hall of Famer Doak Walker for a touchdown.

Down 24–14 in the 4th quarter, Jimmy Finks, in attempting to rally Pittsburgh, tosses a flare pass to running back Fran "Hey Diddle Diddle Rogel Up the Middle" Rogel, who bobbles the pass right to Stits. Stits jogs 7 yards for the clinching touchdown, becoming the last man in league history to throw a touchdown pass and return an interception for a touchdown in the same game.

1994 New England has won just 17 of their previous 76 games and must win to have any chance at the play-offs since they are now 3–6 on the season. The Vikings, with Warren Moon at the helm, have built a 20–3 lead at the half. Drew Bledsoe passes on 59 of the final 66 Patriot plays, and New England wins 26–20 in overtime at Foxboro.

Bledsoe sets league records for passes attempted with 70 and completions with 45. He spreads the ball around to seven different receivers for 426 yards (a team record). Moon and Bledsoe combine to attempt 112 passes without an interception, and there is only 1 sack in the game. These two men go on to lead their respective conferences in attempts, completions, and yards for the season. This victory is the spark the Patriots need, as they continue on to win seven straight and earn a wild card berth to the play-offs.

14

1943 The 6–0–1 Chicago Bears are at the Polo Grounds in New York to take on the 2–2–1 Giants. Sid Luckman sets a new record for touchdown passes in a game with 7, as he completes 21 of 32. Luckman also sets a new standard for yards passing in a game with 433. Luckman spreads his touchdown passes over all four quarters to four different receivers, as the Bears demolish the Giants, 56–7.

The Bear defense limits New York to 157 total yards, while the offense gains 682 yards. This differential was the record at that time. Chicago goes on to return to the championship game yet again and manages to gain revenge for the disappointing 1942 loss to the Redskins. Luckman again plays a superb overall game in bringing the Bears another championship.

At the same time Luckman is torching the Giants, the Redskins are meeting the Lions in our nation's capital. The 4–0–1 defending league champion Redskins are playing host to the 3–4–1 Detroit Lions.

Only one man in the history of the game has ever thrown 4 touchdown passes and intercepted 4 passes in a game—Sammy Baugh. Washington leads 7–0 on a Baugh touchdown pass to Bob Masterson at the end of the 1st quarter. Baugh's 2nd-quarter performance is one for the ages. Lion tailback and future league MVP Frank Sinkwich, on a roll right jump pass, is intercepted by Baugh, who returns the ball into Lion territory. Slingin' Sam completes a 28-yard pass to Bob Seymour for the touchdown.

Art Van Tone is in at tailback for Detroit, and Baugh intercepts his long pass deep in Washington territory. Baugh quick kicks the Redskins out of danger (he does this the entire game). Later, Baugh records his 3rd interception of the quarter, as Washington heads to the locker room leading 21–0.

Baugh directs the Redskins 79 yards on the opening drive of the 3rd quarter. Baugh hits Masterson on a beautifully run corner route for 10 yards and the touchdown. Baugh has intercepted for the 4th time, and now late in the 4th quarter he again directs the Redskins on a sustained drive. He completes a short out on a timing pattern to his favorite receiver, Joe Aguirre, for his 4th and final touchdown pass.

15

1953 The Cleveland Browns have won 32 of their past 37 games and are at home to face San Francisco. The 49ers are again in a tight race with the Lions and Rams for the divisional title. Cleveland's Hall of Fame passing combination of Otto Graham and Dante Lavelli provide the field position as the Browns break on top on a Billy Reynolds toss sweep left as he crawls in the remaining couple of yards.

After a Lou Groza field goal (he has now set a record of scoring in 41 consecutive games), the 49ers drive 77 yards. Hugh "The King" McElhenny bounces outside on a trap left for 33 yards to set up his own 4-yard dive play behind an outstanding drive block from future Hall of Fame offensive tackle Bob St. Clair.

Late in the 2nd quarter comes the most remembered play of the game; Graham, after being knocked out of bounds, is belted in the face by 49er rookie middle guard Art "Boom Boom" Michalik. The Browns start on their own 4-yard line the first time they get the ball in the 3rd quarter with Graham back at quarterback. Graham is now wearing a four-inch clear plastic bar to protect his jaw. After a 15-play drive masterfully led by Graham, Groza puts the Browns ahead 13–7 on his 11-yard field goal.

The teams trade post pattern long pass touchdowns to begin the 4th quarter, the Browns by Ray Renfro and San Francisco by Hugh McElhenny. Late in the 4th quarter with Cleveland ahead, Y. A. Tittle directs the 49ers 84 yards and he himself scores on a bootleg right. Tittle goes on to complete 17 of 27 for 214 yards, while Graham completes 17 of 24 for 286 yards in the 23–21 victory. The 457 total yards gained by the Browns are the most allowed by

San Francisco all season. Cleveland continues on to again play Detroit for the championship.

1959   The first-place New York Giants have lost in Pittsburgh, so with a victory over the Redskins, the Browns can move into a first-place tie. Fullback Jim Brown is again leading the league in rushing (862 yards), yet he is not the key today in the Browns 31–17 victory. His backfield running mate, Bobby Mitchell, is the difference in this game as he gains 232 yards on just 14 carries, including a 90-yard 1st-quarter run. Mitchell does not earn a Pro Bowl berth during the season.

16

1958   The 4–3 Rams are at City Stadium in Green Bay to play the 1–5–1 Packers. Quarterback Bill Wade of Los Angeles passes for the third most yards in Ram history with 372 on just 19 completions (his 2,875 yards passing for the season is second all-time to Sammy Baugh). Los Angeles gains 484 yards in total offense, with the highlight being Jim "Red" Phillips's rookie receiving yardage record of 208 yards. Behind 7–3 in the 1st quarter, Phillips's 93-yard touchdown catch (the longest in team history at this point in time) puts the Rams ahead to stay. The Ram defense is led by left safety Don Burroughs, who, for the second time in his career, intercepts 3 passes in a game.

1969   Tom Landry and his Dallas Cowboys again face Vince Lombardi; this time, however, Lombardi is the head coach of the rival Washington Redskins. Rookie running back Calvin Hill gains 150 yards rushing on 27 carries and scores twice in leading Dallas to a 41–28 victory.

Washington, down 24–7 in the 2nd quarter, rallies behind the passing of future Hall of Fame quarterback Sonny Jurgensen, who passes for 338 yards and 4 touchdowns. The Cowboy pass defense responds to the Jurgensen challenge as they intercept 4 passes. Defensive tackle Larry Cole returns an interception 41 yards for a touchdown (he goes on to return 3 against the Skins in his career). Free safety Mel Renfro "picks off" 2, and finally with Washington down just 34–28, Chuck Howley stops the Redskins with his late 4th-quarter interception.

1980 The 7–3 Houston Oilers and 4–6 Chicago Bears are at Soldier Field in a battle of rushing champions. Earl Campbell and Walter Payton have led their respective conferences in rushing the past two seasons. On this day, however, Campbell wins the war as he gains 206 yards on 31 carries. Payton gains just 60 yards. The Oilers line up for a field goal down 6–0 late in the 2nd quarter. Holder Gifford Nielsen "shovel passes" to Timmy Wilson for the only touchdown of the game in the 10–6 victory. Campbell continues on to win the rushing title again and becomes the first man in league history to record four 200-yard rushing games in a season. Houston again earns a wild card berth in the play-offs.

17

1940 Ace Parker and the 5–3 Brooklyn Dodgers are hosting the Cleveland Rams at Ebbets Field. As he did so many times in his MVP season, Parker leads the Dodgers to victory. Trailing 14–0 in the 2nd quarter, Parker returns a wayward Ram pass 68 yards for a touchdown. Brooklyn dominates play in the 2nd half, as Parker throws 2 touchdown passes. He now is in very select company, returning an interception for a touchdown and throwing a touchdown pass in the same game. Parker goes on to tie for the league lead in interceptions with 6 and direct Jock Sutherland's offense with aplomb as the Dodgers finish second in the Eastern Conference race.

1963　The 2–7 San Francisco 49ers are heading to Yankee Stadium to play the 7–2 contending New York Giants. New York must win to stay in the race with the Cardinals, Steelers, and Browns. New York amasses a season high in total offense of 568 yards in a 48–14 victory.

Y. A. Tittle continues his relentless pursuit of throwing the most touchdown passes in a season, a record he set the previous season. Tittle throws 4 touchdown passes in the game (2 to future Hall of Famer Frank Gifford) and continues on to set the season record with 36. His main target for the past three seasons has been all-league split end Del Shofner. Shofner catches 7 passes for 159 yards and his season long, a 70-yard touchdown. Shofner catches 32 touchdown passes from 1961 through 1963, and amazingly all of them occur in victory.

The Giants running game is in full force against the Niners, as Joe Morrison and Phil King combine to gain 199 yards on 33 carries. For the third time in five seasons, the kickoff return title is won by Abe Woodson of San Francisco. Although at times the Giants attempt to kick away from Abe, he fields a long, bouncing kickoff on his 1-yard line in the 3rd quarter and goes the distance to tie Verda Smith's record of 3 kickoff return touchdowns in a season. At one point in his career, Woodson tallied 22 kickoff returns of 44 yards or longer in the span of just 63 games. No one else in league history comes close to this achievement.

18

1951 The 5–2 Los Angeles Rams are involved in a four-team fight for the National Conference title and for the second time this season are at home in the Coliseum against the hapless 0–6–1 New York Yanks. Pro Bowl halfback George Taliaferro gains 166 yards rushing, including a 65-yard touchdown run. Taliaferro runs for 2 touchdowns and tosses a 20 yarder to Bob Celeri, as the Yanks score all 21 of their points in the 2nd quarter. The Rams lead at halftime, 34–21.

The total offense by both teams is a record-setting 1,133 yards. The Rams "bull elephant" backfield of Dan Towler, Tank Younger, and Dick Hoerner goes on to gain 1,643 yards for the season on just 256 carries (6.4). Towler leads the Ram attack in this game with 155 yards on just 13 carries, including a 69-yard touchdown run in the 2nd quarter. The Yanks, in their last season of football, allow the Rams 102 points and more than 550 yards rushing. The Rams go on to win their only title in Los Angeles.

1973 The 3–5–1 Lions are at Soldier Field to play the 3–6 Bears. Free safety Dick Jauron (an Illinois native) sets the rookie record for yards returned on interceptions with 167 in the 30–7 Detroit victory. Jauron returns a Gary Huff misfire 95 yards for a touchdown in the 2nd quarter. The Lion offense is provided by running back Altie Taylor, who gains 106 yards rushing on 18 carries. The Detroit defense records 4 sacks and intercepts 5 passes. Later in the season, Jauron returns a Bear pass 41 yards, giving him 4 interceptions for the season against Chicago for 208 yards. He later returns to Chicago to become their head football coach and is named NFL coach of the year in 2001.

19

1950 The 6–2 Giants, in a tight divisional race with the Cleveland Browns, journey to Baltimore to take on the 1–7 Colts. On a toss sweep right fullback Jim Spavital of the Colts cuts back to the middle of field and after a 19-yard gain laterals to center Joel Williams, who trundles 50 yards for a touchdown. Achille Maggioli's 38-yard interception return sets up Y. A. Tittle's 15-yard pass to halfback Billy Stone. Later in the 2nd quarter, Tittle lofts a pass down the middle of the field 35 yards to Hal Crisler, who outleaps Emlen Tunnell for the touchdown. Baltimore now leads 20–0. The Giants finally respond as they drive 80 yards in just 7 running plays. Eddie Price sets up his short plunge by earlier running for 38 yards. New York is down 20–7 at the half.

The week before, the Giants scored 51 points against the Cardinals, and much of the offense was provided by using the "A" formation. This week Travis Tidwell is at quarterback in the "T" formation. Eddie Price is at it again, as his 58-yard run sets up a 5-yard bootleg pass by Tidwell to Bob McChesney. The second McChesney touchdown is set up by Tunnell's 36-yard punt return. Travis Tidwell explodes for 54 yards and sets up his quarterback sneak. Jim Ostendarp, Eddie Price, and Randy Clay all score on the ground in the 4th quarter.

The final piece to the Giants team record rushing performance (423 yards) is Robert "Stonewall" Jackson, who scores from 55 yards on a toss sweep left. New York's 55–20 victory propels them to the American Conference play-offs. New York proves to be elusive all season, as a record-setting nine times a Giant runner had a run of 50 yards or longer in leading the league with 2,336 yards rushing.

1961 The league defending champion Houston Oilers start 1–3–1; a coaching change to Wally Lemm ensues. George Blanda goes on to complete 146 of 273 passes for 2,691 yards and 30 touchdowns in a nine-game win streak. The highlight of the win streak is Blanda's record-tying 7-touchdown pass performance against the New York Titans. Receivers Charlie Hennigan and Bill Groman combine for 245 yards on 15 receptions. The Oilers contine on to become the first team to score more than 500 points in a season and also successfully defend their title.

20

1966 For the first time in their seven-year history, the Dallas Cowboys are contending for the Eastern Division title and with a 6–2–1 record are in Pittsburgh to play a 3–5–1 Steeler team. Don Meredith's 38-yard scoring pass to Bob Hayes in the 4th quarter gives Dallas a 20–7 lead. While the Steeler pass rush records 5 sacks, it is the beginning of "Doomsday," as the Cowboys set a league record that still exists as they pillage the Pittsburgh pass pocket 12 times. Dallas goes on to play Green Bay for the right to go to the first Super Bowl.

1977 The 4–5 Bears have not had a winning season in a decade and are at Soldier Field to play divisional rival Minnesota, who is in first place with a record of 6–3. Although Walter Payton has gained 933 yards rushing in his last seven games, that total pales in comparison to his performance today when the Bears needed it the most. The future Hall of Famer gains 144 yards on 26 carries in the 1st half alone, and the Bears lead, 10–0. When Matt Blair returns a blocked punt 10 yards for a touchdown in the 3rd quarter, the Vikes are back in the game.

From this point on in the game, Walter takes his team on his shoulders and gains 129 yards rushing on 14 carries. The key run is a 58-yard blast on a 2nd and 9 from the Bears 21-yard line late in the 4th quarter. Payton establishes a new record for yards gained rushing in a game with 275. Chicago continues to win and earns their first play-off berth in 14 years.

1983 Bill Parcells's first year as a head coach has not gone well, as the Giants are 2–8–1. They are at the Vet in Philadelphia to play the 4–7 Eagles. For the first 11 weeks of the season, Butch Woolfolk has averaged 12 carries for 46 yards, but in this game he gains 159 yards rushing on a record-setting 43 carries. His longest run of the day is 13 yards, and the Giants control the clock for more than 46 minutes. New York's outstanding linebacker corps, led by future Hall of Famers Harry Carson and Lawrence Taylor, limit the Eagles to 10 yards rushing on 9 attempts. "The Big Tuna" (Parcells) has brought his style of football to the Giants in this 23–0 dominating victory.

21

1948 The 2–6 New York Giants take on the 3–6 Packers at Wisconsin State Fair Park. Although the Giants have taken their lumps playing 19 rookies so far in the season, on this day everything goes right in the 49–3 victory. Charlie Conerly throws for 3 touchdowns and runs for another to pace the offense. Future Hall of Fame left safety Emlen Tunnell records the first of four games in his career where he intercepts 3 passes. One of Tunnell's interceptions is a

43-yard touchdown return in the 2nd quarter. The defending league interception champion Frank Reagan records 2 of New York's 8 interceptions.

1954 The 1–7 Cardinals host the 2–6 Washington Redskins at Comiskey Park in Chicago. In another brilliant all-around performance, Ollie Matson proves to be the difference. Tied at 7 in the 2nd quarter, Matson scores on a short pass reception to put the Cardinals ahead to stay. Ollie gains 163 yards rushing on just 8 carries and scores three 2nd-half touchdowns on runs of 62, 15, and 79 (the third longest in team history at that time) in a 38–16 victory.

Matson gains 276 all-purpose yards in this game and does the same the following week in a rematch with Pittsburgh. Earlier in the season, Matson had set the Cardinal record of 284 all-purpose yards in the only other Chicago victory of the season. Matson goes on to be the only Cardinal offensive player chosen for the Pro Bowl in 1954.

1976 The revitalized Cardinals under Don Coryell made the play-offs in both 1974 and 1975. St. Louis, at 8–2, is at home today against the back-to-the-wall 6–4 Washington Redskins under George Allen. Mike Thomas gains the second most yards rushing in Redskin history with 195 on 31 carries as Washington wins this key game, 16–10. Down 7–6 at the half, Thomas's 22-yard touchdown run in the 3rd quarter puts the Skins ahead. The "Over the Hill Gang" continues to win in the next three weeks and makes the play-offs.

22

1942 Don Hutson sets seasonal records for receptions, yards, and touchdowns. Against the Giants he ties the record for most catches in a game with 14 in a 21-all tie with New York.

1945 The 7–1 first-place Cleveland Rams take on the 6–2 Lions at Briggs Stadium on Thanksgiving Day for the Western Division title. Rookie Bob Waterfield completes 12 of 21 passes for 329 yards in his MVP season as the Rams prevail 28–21. Waterfield's main target is left end Jim Benton, who catches 10 passes for a record-setting 303 yards. Benton's sideline reception and 56-yard gain sets up Fred Gehrke's 23-yard scoring run. Benton scores the Ram go-ahead touchdown on a crossing pattern for 70 yards. Although Detroit rallies in the 4th quarter, it is not enough to overcome the yardage gained by Benton on his many key receptions. The Rams go on to win the championship.

1962 The undefeated Packers are in Detroit for the annual Thanksgiving Day clash with the 8–2 Lions. Green Bay's "run to daylight" offense has averaged 183 yards a game rushing. The Lions front seven allow the Pack only 73 yards on the ground. Detroit's blitzing defense records 10 sacks and builds a 23–0 lead.

The Lion offense is paced by team MVP Gail Cogdill, who scores on a 33-yard "up" pattern against future Hall of Famer Willie Wood in the 1st quarter and a 27-yard "corner" route against future Hall of Fame corner Herb Adderley in the 2nd quarter. It is the only Packer loss of the season as they successfully defend their title against the Giants.

1979 The 9–3 Oilers take on the 8–4 Cowboys in a battle for Texas supremacy on Thanksgiving Day. Earl Campbell's 27-yard run in the 2nd quarter cuts the Dallas lead to 21–17. The "Tyler Rose" (Campbell) continues to batter the Cowboys, as he gains the second most yards rushing against them in history with 195 on 33 carries. Houston pulls out the victory, 30–24. Both teams advance to the play-offs.

23

1969 The 8–1 Dallas Cowboys, who have won 42 of their last 54 games, are in the Los Angeles Coliseum to take on the undefeated Rams, who have lost just 5 of their past 42 games. Although they are outgained in the game by Dallas, the Ram defense makes the same key plays they have made all year in winning 24–23. The Rams were +20 in turnover ratio entering the game, and the opposition averaged just 267 yards a game.

The Raiders, at 8–1–1, are taking on the 9–1 rival Chiefs at Municipal Stadium in Kansas City. Oakland has outgained the opposition in every game so far in the season, until today. The difference in the game is the 7 Chief turnovers, including interception returns for a touchdown by George Atkinson and Dan Conners, as the Raiders win, 27–24. Kansas City's main offensive weapon is wide receiver Otis Taylor, who catches 6 for 103 yards.

1975 The 9–0 Minnesota Vikings are hosting the 0–9 San Diego Chargers at Metropolitan Stadium. Fran Tarkenton becomes the all-time completions leader in this game, surpassing John Unitas. Running back Chuck Foreman becomes the first Viking to rush for more than 100 yards for five consecutive games (127 on 33 carries) and scores 3 touchdowns. The last is a 10-yard run to put the game away, 28–13. Tarkenton continues on to finish second in the league in passer rating at 91.8, and Foreman finishes second in the league in yards from scrimmage.

1986   The 9–2 Denver Broncos travel to the Meadowlands to play the 9–2 New York Giants. The Broncos outgain the Giants in the game 405 to 262, and John Elway completes 29 of 48 for 336 yards. Down 6–3 in the 2nd quarter, the Giant defense makes the play of the game, as defensive end George Martin's one-hand interception and 78-yard return for a touchdown turns the game around in New York's 19–16 victory. New York's offense is led by Joe Morris, who gains 106 yards on 23 carries. Morris goes on to set a Giant record with seven 100-yard rushing performances during the season.

24

1946   Detroit's winning teams of 1944 and 1945 are a distant memory in this disastrous 1–10 Lion version of 1946. They are at Wrigley Field to play the 6–1–1 Bears. Detroit is last in the league in running the ball and gains only 27 yards on 15 attempts against the "Monsters of the Midway." The Lions open the scoring with rookie Bob Cifers catching a 47-yard pass from Elmer Madarik. It is all Bears the rest of the game, the final Chicago 42, Detroit 6.

In this game, Cifers sets the record for the highest punting average in a game with 4 punts for 247 yards and his season long of 73. The week before, Cifers had a 66-yard punt against Green Bay. Amazingly, Detroit has a team full of excellent punters, as five different Lions go on to have a punt of 60 yards or longer during the season. Cifers not only finishes first in the league in punting average, but continues to impress as a receiver, with 3 other pass receptions during the season that are all touchdowns.

1949 The Lions are again losing to the contending Bears, this time in Detroit on Thanksgiving. Chicago is ahead 28–0 in the 4th quarter and is passing for more. Robert "Tulsa Bob" Smith intercepts in his own end zone and sets sail 102 yards for a touchdown and a new league record.

1968 The 8–2 Chargers are in a tight divisional battle with the 8–2 Raiders and the 9–2 Chiefs. San Diego is playing host to the 7–3 Jets. Future Hall of Famer Joe Namath pierces the San Diego secondary for 337 yards. The Jet tandem of George Sauer and Don Maynard combine for 11 catches and 290 yards in the 37–15 victory. The lone highlight for the Chargers is Les "Speedy" Duncan, who sets the AFL record for the longest punt return in league history with a 95-yard touchdown return in the 2nd quarter.

1991 The 7–4 Lions are at the Metrodome to take on the 6–6 Vikings. Barry Sanders becomes the first Lion to rush for more than 200 yards in a game (220 on 23 carries) in the 34–14 Detroit victory. Sanders scores 4 touchdowns in the game and goes on to lead the Lions to the NFC title game against the Redskins.

25

1951 George Halas and his 6–2 first-place Chicago Bears are at Municipal Stadium in Cleveland to take on Paul Brown and the 7–1 defending league champion Browns. In recent weeks, the Bear defense has dominated opponents, but not today as "Dub" Jones ties the league record by scoring 6 touchdowns. Jones gains 116 yards rushing on just 9 carries, and his 2 touchdown receptions gain 77 yards. Otto Graham passes for 277 yards on just 12 completions, half of them to Mac Speedie, who gains 144 yards. Down 42–7 in the 4th quarter, "The Claw," otherwise known as Ed Sprinkle, rips Graham's helmet off on a pass rush causing a fumble, which Sprinkle returns 55 yards for a touchdown.

1974   The first-place Steelers, at 7–2–1, take a trip to the bayou and Tulane Stadium to play the 4–6 New Orleans Saints. Terry Bradshaw again struggles with his passing as he gains only 80 yards on his 19 attempts, yet he has his best day ever running the ball (99 yards on 9 carries).

Bud Carson's defense continues to shine in the 28–7 victory as they allow just 69 yards net passing due to a pass rush that records 6 sacks. Hall of Fame linebacker Jack Ham records an interception and makes plays all over the field.

Rookie Lynn Swann returns a punt 64 yards for a touchdown in the 3rd quarter to put Pittsburgh ahead, 21–7. The Steelers enjoy the game at Tulane Stadium on national television so much they plan to return there in January. The key for Pittsburgh is the outstanding performance by the offensive line and future Hall of Fame running back Franco Harris, as he gains 114 yards on 19 carries.

1979   It is the same calendar date, different year as Franco Harris, six years to the day, again gains more than 100 yards, this time against contending division rival Cleveland. The 8–4 Browns are at Three Rivers Stadium, and Brian Sipe keeps Cleveland in the game with 333 yards passing on his 23 completions and 3 touchdowns. Terry

Bradshaw throws for a career high 364 yards on his 30 completions. Franco Harris and Rocky Bleier gain 333 yards rushing and receiving, while L. C. Greenwood keys the defense with 4 of the Steelers 7 sacks in the 33–30 overtime victory.

26

1961 The 2–8 Oakland Raiders are in the Cotton Bowl to play the 3–7 Dallas Texans, who have lost six straight games. Durable all-league halfback Abner Haynes (who never missed a game with the Texans/Chiefs) is the first player in AFL history to score 5 touchdowns in a game, as the Texans win 43–11. Haynes gains 158 yards rushing on just 14 carries and has touchdown runs of 33 and 27 yards. He also scores on a 66-yard reception from Cotton Davidson. Haynes continues on to lead the AFL in rushing touchdowns for three consecutive years (1960–1962).

The 4–6 St. Louis Cardinals are in Pittsburgh against the 4–6 Steelers. Left safety Jerry Norton of the Cards intercepts Bobby Layne's sideline pass and scoots down the sideline 47 yards for a touchdown. Pittsburgh rallies and takes a 27–13 lead into the 4th quarter. John David Crow closes the gap to 7 on a touchdown reception, and then with his 4th interception of the day, Jerry Norton scores from 37 yards out.

Norton joins that select group of men who have returned 2 interceptions for a touchdown in a game, and he is also the only player to record 4 interceptions in a game twice. Norton has now intercepted 16 passes in his last 17 games. The Steelers rally late in the 4th quarter to pull out a 30–27 victory.

1989 The 7–4 Rams are in Superdome to play the 6–5 Saints. With just under three minutes to play, New Orleans has a 17–3 lead, but Willie "Flipper" Anderson sets up one Ram touchdown with a 46-yard reception and scores the other from 15 yards out to put the game into overtime.

Anderson sets up the game-winning field goal with a 26-yard reception. By gaining 336 yards receiving in the game, he establishes a new record (he gains 251 yards in the 2nd half and overtime). Los Angeles goes on to win five of their next six games and play San Francisco for the right to go to the Super Bowl.

27

1949 The defending 8–1 league champion Eagles are at home to face the 5–3–1 Steelers. The Steeler single-wing attack gains a season low 62 yards rushing, while Philadelphia picks up 486 yards in total offense (the most allowed by Pittsburgh all year).

Future Hall of Famer Steve Van Buren records his seventeenth 100-yard rushing game as the Eagles win, 34–17. Van Buren, with 205 yards, becomes just the second player in league history to gain more than 200 yards rushing in a game. Philadelphia goes on to defend its crown with another title game shutout, and Van Buren provides the offense with another outstanding rushing performance.

1966 The Redskins, at 5–6, are hosting the 1–8–1 Giants. New York gains 389 yards in total offense and scores 6 offensive touchdowns; however, the 41 points are not near enough as Washington scores 10 touchdowns in the 72–41 victory. The future Hall of Fame passing combination of Sonny Jurgensen (10 of 16 for 145) and Charlie

Taylor (6 catches for 124 yards and 2 TDs) does its usual fine work, yet it is youngsters A. D Whitfield and Brig Owens in their first years as Redskins that are the highlight of the game.

Whitfield scores his only 3 touchdowns of the season, and Owens intercepts 3 passes. Owens returns a Giant fumble 62 yards for a touchdown and an interception in the 4th quarter 60 yards for a touchdown. New York stumbles on to set the record for most points allowed in a season with 501.

1988 The 9–3 Bengals, at Riverfront Stadium, are hosting the 11–1 Buffalo Bills in the AFC title game preview. Ickey Woods's 2-yard touchdown run in the 4th quarter clinches the 35–21 victory for Cincinnati. Woods gains 129 yards on 26 carries and scores 3 touchdowns (he now has 13 in 13 games). The Bengal offense purrs as they ring up 440 yards in total offense. The victory is a turning point for both teams, as the Bengals earn home field advantage in the play-offs.

28

1929 Hall of Famer Ernie Nevers scores all 40 points by the Cardinals in their victory over the Bears. Nevers is the first man to score 6 touchdowns in a game.

1948 The 6–3 Washington Redskins invade Wrigley Field to take on the 8–1 Chicago Bears. The Bears must continue to win to keep pace with the champion Cardinals. The Skins are already trailing in the 1st quarter 7–0 when they try a toss sweep left, but when Bob Nussbaumer is hit by the Bears right defensive end Ed Cifers, he fumbles.

Bears right corner Fred "Dippy" Evans scoops up the ball and scampers 10 yards for a touchdown.

On the next series, Washington tries an inside running play to rookie Howard Hartley, who is stripped of the ball by Bears defensive tackle Walt Stickel. The ball bounces up off the ground into the waiting hands of Evans, who trots 16 yards into the end zone. Evans, who plays in only 3 games in his NFL career, sets a record that still stands today as the only player in league history to return 2 fumbles for a touchdown in a game. Chicago goes on to a decisive win, 48–13.

1965 The 5–5 49ers are taking on the 5–5 Vikings at Metropolitan Stadium. Rookie Ken Willard records his first 100-yard rushing performance (113 on 18 carries), yet the star of the day is John Brodie, as he passes for 209 yards on just 10 completions. Four different 49ers catch his 5 touchdown passes in this 45–24 San Francisco victory. Brodie continues on to complete 145 of 223 passes for 1,843 yards and 20 touchdowns in the games the Niners won or tied as he earns his first Pro Bowl berth. With a passer rating of 95.3, he finishes second to John Unitas for the season in this all-important category.

1993 The 7–3 49ers are traveling to Anaheim to play the 3–7 Rams. Steve Young completes 26 of 32 for 462 yards (the second most in team history) and 4 touchdowns in a 35–10 victory. Jerry Rice and John Taylor combine for 316 yards on 14 receptions and 3 touchdowns. Young becomes the first quarterback in league history to win the passing title with a rating of more than 100 for three consecutive years. San Francisco returns to the NFC title game.

29

1964 The 6–5 Vince Lombardi–led Packers travel to the Cotton Bowl to play the 4–6–1 Tom Landry–led Cowboys. Dallas, down 10–0 in the 2nd quarter, has the ball at the Packer 24. Right outside Lee Roy Caffey blitzes quarterback John Roach, and the forced fumble is returned 60 yards for a touchdown by future Hall of Fame defensive tackle Henry Jordan.

The Cowboys respond with two 2nd-quarter touchdowns. The first is a 69-yard punt return by rookie free safety Mel Renfro and the second a short run by Billy Lothridge after a long sustained drive.

Green Bay's defense shines all afternoon as Dallas gains only 132 yards in total offense. Hall of Fame linebacker Ray Nitschke records 2 interceptions, and in the 4th quarter right defensive end Lionel Aldridge returns a Perry Lee Dunn fumble 29 yards for a touchdown to put the Packers ahead, 45–14.

Late in the 4th quarter, Hall of Fame running back Paul Hornung loses 5 yards on a sweep and fumbles. Cornerback Warren Livingston of the Cowboys returns the ball 17 yards for a touchdown. This is the first game in league history where 3 opponent fumbles are returned for a touchdown. Future Hall of Famer Mel Renfro sets a record for combined kick returns in a game. Renfro returns 8 kickoffs for 156 yards and 4 punts for 117 yards.

1970 At Memorial Stadium in Baltimore, the 7–2–1 Colts, coming off a disappointing loss to the Dolphins, take on their old rivals, the 4–6 Chicago Bears. The Butkus-led defense intercepts 5 John Unitas passes and builds up a 17–0 2nd-quarter lead. The Colt ground attack is sputtering, so Johnny U. just keeps passing. He spreads the ball out to Roy Jefferson, Eddie Hinton, Tom Mitchell, and Sam Havrilak for 17 completions and 165 yards.

It is now late in the 4th quarter, and Baltimore still trails 20–14. Hall of Fame tight end John Mackey has caught 4 short passes in the game so far, but with the game on the line Unitas hits Mackey deep in Bear territory for 54 yards and the winning touchdown. Unitas continues on to complete his 15th season with his one and only Super Bowl ring.

30

1947 Don Currivan played in 39 games in his four years in the NFL with some success as a deep threat catching the ball. He caught 39 passes for 901 yards and 9 touchdowns. The 3–5–1 Boston Yanks are playing host to the 3–6 Redskins, and Currivan establishes a league record for yards per catch in a game with 3 receptions for 181 yards. Trailing 17–13 in the 3rd quarter, Currivan scores on a 67-yard pass from Boley Dancewicz to put the Yanks back in the lead. Boston prevails in the game, 27–24.

Currivan goes on to average an impressive 32.6 yards per catch for the 1947 season. During the 1948 season, he is traded to Los Angeles. When Los Angeles wins the division title in 1949 (Currivan's last season), he is a fixture in the revamped Ram secondary.

1987 In the Kingdome, the 7–3 Seahawks are hosting the 3–7 Raiders. Deep in their own territory with a 14–7 lead in the 2nd quarter, rookie Bo Jackson explodes for 91 yards on a sweep left behind a Marcus Allen block. Jackson establishes a new Raider record for yards gained rushing in a game with 221. The Raiders romp to victory, 37–14, as they gain 356 yards rushing as a team. Jackson continues on to average 6.8 yards per carry for the season.

1997 The first-place 10–2 Broncos are in San Diego to play the 4–8 Chargers. Although the John Elway to Ed Mc-Caffrey passing combination has a fine day for Denver, the game belongs to Terrell Davis as he gains 178 yards rushing. For the tenth time, Davis records a 100-yard rushing game (a Bronco record) in the season. Davis goes on to finish second to Barry Sanders for the rushing title. With a 21–7 lead in the 2nd quarter, safety Steve Atwater returns an interception 22 yards for a touchdown to give Denver an insurmountable lead. This is the fifth time during this Super Bowl season that the Broncos have had a 100-yard rusher (Davis) and have returned an interception for a touchdown—all victories—a team record that still stands.

December

1

1940 As a rookie in 1939, Davey O'Brien set the league record for completions in a game. Sammy Baugh broke his record in November of 1940. Now, in his last game as a pro, O'Brien establishes records for both attempts (60) and completions (33) in a 13–6 loss to the Eastern Division champion Redskins. O'Brien gains 316 yards passing (which remains an Eagle team record for 13 years) and 1 touchdown. He is not intercepted in the game. He completes 14 passes for 180 yards to Don Looney (the league record for most receptions in a game) and on defense contributes a 51-yard interception return.

1963 The 8–3 Browns are invading St. Louis to take on the 8–3 Cardinals in a game where the loser is virtually eliminated from the Eastern Division race. Cleveland avenges an earlier home loss to the Cardinals, as Jim Brown sets a new league record for yards rushing in a season in a 24–10 victory. Brown gains 179 yards on 29 carries to bring his season total to 1,677 (in 1958 he gained 1,527) and scores two 2nd-quarter rushing touchdowns.

1968 The 7–4 Giants are in Municipal Stadium in Cleveland to play the 8–3 Browns. Leading 17–3 entering the 3rd quarter, future Hall of Famer Leroy Kelly runs for 3 touchdowns in the 2nd half as the Browns win 45–10 to remain in contention with the Cardinals in the Century Division.

The last touchdown in the game by Cleveland is scored by reserve wide receiver Tommy McDonald (the last touchdown of his career) on a 12-yard pass from Frank Ryan. Now in his 12th and final season, McDonald still brings his enthusiasm, as well as his helmet without a face mask.

In the first 50 years of the NFL, he is second on the all-time list to Don Hutson with 84 touchdown receptions. Six times Hutson caught at least 3 touchdown passes in a game (McDonald had 5). This future Hall of Famer goes on to gain 8,410 yards receiving, and 39 times he caught a touchdown pass of 30 yards or longer.

2

1951 Future Hall of Famer Elroy "Crazy Legs" Hirsch has caught 64 passes in his two-year career entering the 1951 season (he goes on to catch 66 passes this season). He plays opposite a record-setting receiver in Tom Fears and catches passes from two future Hall of Fame quarterbacks.

The 6–3 Rams are at Wrigley Field to play the 6–3 Bears. In the Rams six victories, Hirsch has caught 32 passes for 816 yards and 10 touchdowns. His 91-yard touchdown in the 1st quarter cuts the Bear lead in half, as the Rams go on to win 42–17 (Hirsch catches 3 passes for

106 yards). Hirsch continues on to set numerous records during the season (yards receiving and consecutive-games touchdown receptions) in the Rams quest for a title.

1962 The 8–3 Oilers need to win to stay ahead of the 8–3–1 Patriots and are facing the 7–5 Broncos at home in Jeppesen Stadium. The teams combine to attempt 97 passes in the game and also combine to intercept 13 passes (still the league record). Houston leads 17–14 at the half due to George Blanda's 2 touchdown passes to Billy Cannon (107 yards on 5 catches). All-AFL left corner Tony Banfield and left safety Jim Norton combine to record 4 of the Oilers 8 interceptions, yet the key interception is by all-league defensive end Don Floyd, who returns his interception 28 yards for a touchdown in the 4th quarter to clinch the victory, 34–17.

1979 The 6–7 Vikings are in the Coliseum to play the 7–6 Rams. Tommy Kramer completes 21 passes for 297 yards and 3 touchdowns as Minnesota rallies to tie the game at 21 in the 4th quarter. Free safety Paul Krause of the Vikings intercepts twice to become the all-time interception leader with 81 (Emlen Tunnell previously held the record with 79 for 27 years). Ram safety Nolan Cromwell runs 5 yards on a fake field goal attempt (he is the holder) in overtime to win the game.

2001 The Ravens defeat the visiting Colts 39–27 as safety Rod Woodson returns a Peyton Manning pass 47 yards for a touchdown. This future Hall of Famer has now returned 10 interceptions for a touchdown (all in victory) to break Ken Houston's 30-year-old record (he goes on to return 2 more interceptions for a touchdown as a Raider after he leaves the Ravens).

3

1950 The 6–4 Eagles are at Municipal Stadium to battle the 8–2 Browns (who are tied for first with the Giants). The muddy field conditions and Coach Paul Brown's belief that he could run the ball (no pass attempts and only 69 yards rushing the entire game) and win are the key elements in this historically significant game.

On the third play of the game, Steve Van Buren goes in motion to the right and runs a quick out pattern. Left corner Warren Lahr cuts in front of Van Buren and returns the interception 30 yards for a touchdown (Lahr goes on to become the first modern-era player to return 5 interceptions for a touchdown in a career and amazingly does it in just 45 games).

Dom Moselle's punt return (the teams set a record with 17 combined punt returns) sets up Lou Groza's 35-yard 2nd-quarter field goal to give Cleveland a 10–0 halftime lead. Cleveland goes on to lead the league in pass defense efficiency (28.7) and total defense (247 yards a game) and continually stops the defending league champion Eagles in the 13–7 victory.

1961 Boston, standing at 6–4–1, leads 14–10 in the 3rd quarter and punts to Bob McNamara, who returns the ball 8 yards and reverses the ball to Al Frazier for 55 yards and a touchdown for the 3–9 Broncos. The Patriots reclaim the lead in the 4th quarter and kickoff to Frazier, who goes 90 yards for a touchdown (Frazier becomes just the third player in pro football history to return a punt and a kickoff for a touchdown in the same game). The Patriots prevail, 28–24.

The 3–8 Rams are taking on the 2–9 Vikings at the Met. Rookie Fran Tarkenton sets a league record by completing 13 consecutive passes (late in the 2nd quarter to early in the 4th quarter) in the Vikings 42–21 victory. Tarkenton completes 21 of 30 passes for 252 yards and 4 touchdowns (1 in each quarter). His main target is Pro Bowl receiver Jerry Reichow, with 112 yards on 6 catches.

1967 San Francisco, at 5–6, is hosting the 5–6 Bears at Kezar Stadium. Future Hall of Famer Gale Sayers returns the opening kickoff 97 yards for a touchdown. Sayers returns a 3rd quarter 49er punt 58 yards for a touchdown (he becomes just the fourth man to return both a punt and kickoff for a touchdown in the same game) in the Bears 28–14 victory.

4

1949 A New York Bulldog in the record book? The 1–8–1 Bulldogs are in Detroit to play the 2–8 Lions. End Ralph Heywood becomes just the fourth man in league history to catch 14 passes in a game (he gains 151 yards). Trailing 21–14 in the 4th quarter, Bobby Layne throws 2 touchdowns to Heywood as the Bulldogs take the lead, 27–21.

Detroit comes back to win the game 28–27 on a Frank Tripucka to John Greene pass. Heywood continues his fine play in the final game of the season against Pittsburgh (and the final game of his career) and finishes eighth in the league with 37 receptions.

1955 Entering the game, Cleveland has beaten Pittsburgh 10 of the 11 times they have played. We are at Forbes Field to witness the clash between the 7–2–1 league defending champion Browns and the 4–6 Steelers (who have lost five straight). Fred Morrison triggers the Cleveland offense as he gains 104 yards rushing on just 13 carries in the 30–7 victory. The Browns allow a season low 26 yards rushing (16 carries) as they establish themselves as the best defense in football.

During their championship seasons of 1954 and 1955, Cleveland allows just 20 offensive touchdowns in their 17 victories (6 rushing and 14 passing). The Browns allow an average of just 82 yards rushing in those 17 wins. Nine different Cleveland defenders on the team go on to earn a Pro Bowl berth at some point in their career.

1960   The 5–4 49ers are in the Coliseum to battle with the 3–5–1 Rams. The 49er defense has improved during the season due to the play of their young secondary led by left safety Dave Baker (who earned a Pro Bowl berth as a rookie in 1959). San Francisco defeats Los Angeles 23–7, as Baker becomes just the tenth man in league history to intercept 4 passes in a game. Twice his interceptions lead to field goals, and his two 4th-quarter interceptions on passes intended for Jim "Red" Phillips (8 catches for 114 yards) seal the win. Baker also establishes a record that still stands today, as he has now intercepted 9 passes in his last three games (he continues on to tie Jerry Norton of the Cardinals for the interception title with 10).

5

1948   The 4–6 Giants are at Forbes Field to play the 3–7 Steelers. Rookie Charlie Conerly of New York sets a league record for completions in a game with 36 (he attempts 53 passes) for 363 yards. George Papach leads the Steeler single wing attack as he gains a season high 148 yards on 17 carries (he gains only 324 all year) in a 38–28 victory.

The 9–1 defending league champion Cardinals are in Comiskey Park to tangle with the 3–8 Packers. Chicago and Green Bay combine to run the ball a league record 108 times in the game (Cardinals 70 and Green Bay 38). Tied at 7 in the 2nd quarter, the Cardinals drive 55 yards in 13 plays (12 rushing) to take a 14–7 lead on Paul Christman's 1-yard dive. On their 2nd drive of the 3rd quarter, the Cardinals drive 44 yards on 10 plays (all rushing) to score on Pat Harder's 1-yard run.

Chicago gains 112 yards rushing in the 1st half and 177 in the 2nd as they continually grind out yards against the Packer forward wall. Eleven different Cardinals carry the ball, yet their three main ball carriers remain Elmer Angsman (11 carries for 37 yards), Pat Harder (16 carries for 63 yards), and Charlie Trippi (16 carries for 80 yards). Chicago averages 222 yards a game rushing in their 11 victories (they led the league with 2,560).

Jerry Davis's 29-yard run late in the 4th quarter is the Cardinals longest run of the game. Green Bay completes just 1 pass in the entire game (in the 4th quarter) as Chicago crushes the Packers 42–7 to remain in contention with the crosstown Bears for the division title.

1971 The 6–4–1 Rams are hosting the 4–5–2 Saints in the Coliseum. Willie Ellison gains 247 yards rushing (26 carries) to set a new league record in the 45–28 victory. Ellison starts the scoring with an 80-yard sprint through the Saints defense. Later in the 1st quarter, Travis Williams of the Rams ties a team record with a 105-yard kickoff return for a touchdown. The Ram defense allows the Saints only 56 yards rushing on 23 carries for the entire game.

6

1969 The 8–4 Jets are in the Astrodome to play the 5–5–2 Oilers in a divisional battle. Joe Namath completes just 6 of 16 passes for 52 yards, yet New York builds a 34–10 lead in the 4th quarter. The Jet defense, led by Gerry Philbin and John Elliott, is the difference in this game, as they record 9 sacks (the second most in team history) and intercept 6 passes. Rookie wide receiver Jerry LeVias gains 329 all-purpose yards (only the second player in AFL history to gain more than 300 in a game), including 110 receiving in the 34–26 loss to the Jets.

1970 The 4–7 Redskins are in the Cotton Bowl to play the 7–4 Cowboys, who need to win to keep pace with the division-leading Cardinals. Rookie Duane Thomas glides, cuts, and weaves his way to 123 yards rushing on 19 carries in the 34–0 victory. Dallas's depth is demonstrated as Calvin Hill and Walt Garrison combine to gain 120 yards rushing on 21 carries, yet the 2 Cowboy rushing touchdowns are scored by Dan Reeves.

When Dallas wins, they allow just 95 yards a game rushing. When they lose, they allow 175 yards a game. Washington's Larry Brown does not play today, and the Dallas defense allows the Redskins just 67 yards rushing.

Quarterback Sonny Jurgensen has thrown 19 touchdown passes in his last nine games, but today against "Doomsday" he gains just 110 yards on his 14 completions. Future Hall of Fame defensive backs Mel Renfro and

Herb Adderley both intercept Jurgensen to help keep the Skins out of the end zone.

1998 The 2–10 Colts are in the Georgia Dome to play the 10–2 Falcons. The Colts are unbeaten in their history against Atlanta (10–0) and are tied at 21 at the half. Running back Jamal Anderson enters this game having gained more than 100 yards eight times so far this season (all Falcon victories), and today he continues his relentless assault on opposing defenses as he gains 122 yards on 30 carries in the 28–21 victory. Anderson goes on to set a season record with 1,846 yards rushing for this Atlanta team of destiny.

7

1947 The 7–3 Cardinals are in Philadelphia to battle the 7–3 Eagles. Both teams are embroiled in tough divisional races, and at the half Philadelphia leads 7–3 on a Steve Van Buren 4-yard touchdown run. Chicago gains 185 yards rushing against a Philadelphia defense that allows just 111 a game, while the Cardinal defense limits Van Buren to just 44 in the game.

One of the finest two-way players of his era excels in this game, as Mal Kutner returns an interception 56 yards down the right sideline for a touchdown and later catches a 21-yard scoring pass (dragging two Eagles into the end zone with him) in the 45–21 victory.

1958 The 1–8–1 Packers are at Kezar Stadium to play the 4–6 49ers. San Francisco gains 468 yards in total offense in the 48–21 victory, yet the key figure in this game is right safety Bobby Dan Dillon of Green Bay. In the 3rd quarter on a 2nd and 13 play at the 49er 18, John Brodie throws deep to Fred Dugan. Dillon intercepts and returns the ball 32 yards.

Dillon has now intercepted 47 passes in his last 66 games. He now ranks second to Emlen Tunnell on the all-time interception list with 51. Dillon has returned interceptions more than 100 yards for a record-setting six consecutive seasons. He has also intercepted more Colt, Lion, and Bear passes than any other player in history.

1968 The 1–11–1 Bills are in the Astrodome taking on the 5–7 Oilers. Buffalo gains just 89 yards (a season low) in total offense on 64 plays. Left corner Miller Farr of the Oilers returns interceptions off of Dan Darragh 52 and 40 yards for touchdowns in the 4th quarter (he is the only player in AFL history to return 2 interceptions for a touchdown in a game) in a 35–6 Houston victory.

1997 The 10–3 defending Super Bowl champion Packers are in Tampa for the first-place divisional showdown with the 9–4 Buccaneers. Brett Favre completes 25 of 33 for 280 yards to provide the offense for Green Bay. The Packer defense limits Buccaneer quarterbacks to 10 of 26 passing and registers 4 sacks in the 17–6 victory.

8

1940 For the second time in four years, the Bears are meeting the Redskins for the title. Chicago becomes the "monsters of the midway" today as they wallop Washington, 73–0. The talented (six future Hall of Famers) and young (11 rookies) Bears gain 382 yards rushing on 53 carries as a team.

Sid Luckman runs his version of the "T" formation to perfection and completes 4 of 6 passes for 102 yards. Since the Bears led 28–0 at the half, they knew that the Skins would have to throw on virtually every down to get back in the game. Chicago intercepts 8 of the 51 passes Washington attempts, and more importantly they return 3 of those interceptions for touchdowns. What would the Bears do for an encore?

1963 The 3–9 Redskins are in Yankee Stadium trying to derail the 9–3 Giants. New York must win to keep pace with three other tough Eastern Division teams. Although Washington takes an early lead, the Giants defense is the answer today as they register 5 sacks and take the ball away from the Skins 10 times in the 44–14 victory. All-pro right corner Dick Lynch puts the Giants ahead for the first time in the game when he returns a Snead pass 42 yards for a touchdown (he is the first NFL player to return 3 interceptions for a touchdown in a season).

The 5–5–1 Jets are in Buffalo to battle the 5–6–1 Bills. Cookie Gilchrist sets AFL records for yards gained rushing (243), carries (36), and touchdowns (5) in the Bills 45–14 victory. The bruising Bills defense limits the Jets to just 38 yards rushing as Buffalo moves into play-off contention.

1973 The 10–2 Vikings are at Lambeau Field to take on the 4–6–2 defending NFC Central Division champion Packers. Minnesota leads 7–0 in the 1st quarter, and when quarterback Jerry Tagge throws a quick slant on a 2nd down and 7 situation at his own 38-yard line, right corner Bobby Bryant intercepts and returns 46 yards for a touchdown. Bryant also intercepts on back-to-back Packer drives in the 3rd quarter in the 31–7 Viking victory. Bryant is still the all-time nemesis in Green Bay history as he went on to intercept 13 Packer passes for 213 yards.

9

1934 The undefeated Chicago Bears are at the Polo Grounds in a championship rematch with the Giants. The Bears have overwhelmed many an opponent during the season with their powerful ground attack (2,847 yards). Chicago's defense has allowed just 11 offensive touchdowns in 13 games.

Chicago, led by future Hall of Famer Bronko Nagurski's bruising runs (68 yards), lead 13–3 going into the 4th quarter on an icy field. To combat the conditions, New York dons "sneakers" in the 2nd half and stages a 4th quarter rally. Ed Danowski completes a 28-yard touchdown pass to Ike Frankian to cut the Bear lead to 3. Future Hall of Famer Ken Strong sweeps 42 yards on the next Giant series, and New York has the lead, 17–13.

The Giant defense, led by Mel Hein and Bill Morgan, stonewalls the Bears, and here comes Strong and Danowski again. Strong scores from the 11-yard line on a reverse. Bo Molenda intercepts for the Giants and laterals to Dale Burnett, who scampers to the Chicago 21. Danowski scores from the 9-yard line after 4 straight carries, and the rally is complete, New York 30, Chicago 13.

1945 The Redskins defeat the Giants 17–0 at Griffith Stadium to clinch the Eastern Division crown. For the season, Sammy Baugh completes 102 of 136 for 1,412 yards and 9 touchdowns (with only 2 interceptions) in Washington's eight victories (he played in all ten games, which has never been correctly credited).

1962 The 1–10–1 Rams are traveling to Wrigley Field to take on the 7–5 Chicago Bears (who have won only twice at home all season). Future Hall of Fame tight end Mike Ditka catches 5 passes for 130 yards in the 1st half, including a 1st-quarter touchdown to help propel the Chicago offense. (The Bears lead 23–7 at the half.)

It is the 4th quarter, and the Rams have 4th and goal on the Chicago 4-yard line as former Bear Zeke Bratkowski fires toward the end zone, where Pro Bowl strong safety Richie Petitbon snags the errant pass and sails 101 yards for a Bear record (he is the fifth player in league history to return an interception 100 yards or longer) in a 30–14 victory.

10

1939 We are at Wisconsin State Fair Park in Milwaukee to watch the defending league champion Giants again take on Green Bay for the championship. The Packers drive 47 yards in the 1st quarter to go ahead 7–0 on Arnie Herber's 7-yard pass to Milt Gantenbein. Late in the 1st half, the Giants have the ball on the Packer 14, when rookie linebacker Charley Brock intercepts Ed Danowski's 1st-down pass.

Leading 10–0 in the 3rd quarter, Gantenbein intercepts Danowski and returns the ball to the New York 33. It is 3rd down, and Cecil Isbell lofts a pass to Joe Laws for 31 yards and a touchdown. New York gains just 6 yards in total offense in the 3rd quarter (and is 1 of 6 passing). Green Bay continues to stop New York and has the ball on the Giant 15 after an Earl Svendsen interception of a Len Barnum pass. Four running plays later, Ed Jankowski punches it in from a yard out, and the Packers lead, 27–0.

1961 The 8–3–1 defending AFL champion Oilers are at the Polo Grounds to take on the contending 7–5 Titans. Since the Patriots are now 8–4–1 (they won the day before), Houston must win to keep pace. Halfback Billy Cannon scores 5 touchdowns and gains a league record 373 combined net yards in the game. Cannon catches touchdown passes of 67 and 15 yards (he catches 5 passes for 114 yards in the game) from George Blanda in the 1st half as the Oilers lead 20–7.

Houston sends Cannon in motion out of a triple wing set more than once in the 2nd half, and behind excellent blocking he breaks free for touchdown runs of 61 and 52 yards (he gains 216 yards rushing on 25 carries). With two minutes left in the game, Cannon plows over from 2 yards out as Houston defeats the Titans, 48–21.

1995 The 6–7 Seahawks are at Mile High Stadium to battle the 7–6 Broncos. Glyn Milburn breaks a 34-year-old record for most combined net yards. Milburn, for the only time in his career, gains more than 100 yards rushing in a game, as he totals 131 on 18 carries. He also catches 5 passes for 45 yards and returns kicks for 228 yards (punts 5 for 95 yards and kickoffs 5 for 133 yards). Milburn's 404 yards is impressive but not enough as Seattle overcomes the 20–3 Bronco halftime lead to rally in the 2nd half to win, 31–27.

11

1949 The 8–3 Bears must win at Wrigley Field against the Cardinals and have the Rams lose to win the division title. The 6–4–1 Cardinals have denied the Bears the division title the past two seasons. Bears quarterback Johnny

Lujack has already set a team record by completing 29 passes in a game earlier in the season. Lujack completes 24 of 39 for a team record 468 yards and 6 touchdowns in the 52–21 victory over the Cardinals.

For just the second time in team history, Bear teammates catch passes for more than 100 yards in a game. Rookie John Hoffman and veteran Ken Kavanaugh combine to catch 14 passes for 311 yards and 4 of the touchdowns. The bruising Bear run defense does their job as the Cardinals gain just 48 yards rushing (the Bears led the league in this category by allowing just 99 yards a game for the season). The Rams do indeed win their game, thus denying the Bears the division title.

1955   Only one player in league history has ever won the receiving title three consecutive years and then retired; that man is Pete Pihos. The 7–4 Bears are hosting the 4–6–1 Eagles at Wrigley Field. Chicago must win and have the Rams lose to claim the Western Division title.

After catching 35 passes for 520 yards in his first nine games of the season, Pihos really turns it on in the final three games of his career, as he catches 27 passes for 344 yards. The league-leading Bear ground attack, led by rookie Pro Bowl fullback Rick Casares (79 yards on just 7 carries), is the difference in the 17–10 victory, as they gain 214 yards rushing as a team. The Rams win to deny the Bears the division title once again.

1960   The 3–6–1 Rams not only defeat the 6–4 Colts, but keep a John Unitas receiver out of the end zone. During Johnny's 47-game streak (still the record today), he completed 697 of 1,298 passes for 10,645 yards, while throwing 102 touchdown passes (with just 61 interceptions). In the game, Lenny Moore and Raymond Berry combine to catch just 4 passes for 50 yards, as Unitas completes 17 of 38 for only 182 yards in the 10–3 Ram victory.

12

1937 The Bears are hosting the Redskins at Wrigley Field for the championship. Jack Manders scores all the Bear points in the 1st half as Chicago leads 14–10. Rookie Sammy Baugh gains a record 335 yards passing on 18 completions and 3 touchdowns as Washington rallies in the 2nd half to win the Redskins' first title, 28–21.

1964 The 9–3–1 Browns have the opportunity to clinch their first division title in seven years against bitter rival New York. Frank Ryan completes 12 of 13 passing (Paul Warfield gains 103 yards receiving on 5 catches) for 5 touchdowns in Cleveland's dominant 52–20 performance. The Browns defense registers 4 sacks and 4 takeaways in their contribution to the win.

1965 The 4–8 Eagles are taking on the 2–10 Steelers at Pitt Stadium before just 22,000 fans. Philadelphia ties the 1943 Packer record of 9 interceptions (172 yards) in a game as they humble Pittsburgh 47–13. Jimmy Nettles leads the parade with 3 interceptions for 84 yards (including a 56-yard touchdown return in the 2nd quarter), while Maxie Baughan (33 yards) and former Steeler George Tarasovic (40 yards) return their interceptions for touchdowns to tie another league record.

Marv Woodson of Pittsburgh returns an interception 61 yards for a touchdown in the 3rd quarter to set another record (the most touchdowns on interceptions in a game).

Steeler quarterback Tommy Wade attempts only 66 passes all season yet throws 13 interceptions (7 in this game).

The 8–4 contending Bears are hosting the 7–5 49ers at Wrigley Field. Rookie Gale Sayers scores 6 touchdowns (tying the league record) in a 61–20 demolition of San Francisco, in which they gain 584 yards in total offense. Rudy Bukich throws for a career high 347 yards (16 completions) and starts the scoring avalanche with an 80-yard screen pass to Sayers for touchdown number 1. Sayers scores his next 4 touchdowns on the ground (113 yards rushing on just 9 carries) on a variety of runs. Sayers scores his record-setting 21st touchdown (the most ever in a season) on an 85-yard sprint and cut left on a punt return in the mud. The "Kansas Comet" is the first rookie to amass more than 300 combined yards in a game (336 on 17 plays) and is seventh overall.

13

1953 The 9–2 defending league champion Lions are at the Polo Grounds to take on the 3–8 Giants in Coach Steve Owens's last game. Pro Bowl halfback Frank Gifford catches a touchdown pass and throws a touchdown pass, but it is not enough as Detroit wins 27–16 to clinch the division title.

Bobby Layne completes 17 of 28 passes for 212 yards and 2 touchdowns (to Leon Hart and Doak Walker), and the Lion ground game pounds out 147 yards. Detroit's defense is led by first-time Pro Bowl safeties Yale Lary and Jack Christiansen (both record interceptions), as the Lions lead the league in pass defense efficiency (37.6)

The 5–6 Steelers are at Griffith Stadium to play the 6–4–1 Redskins in Coach Earl "Curly" Lambeau's and halfback Bill Dudley's last game. Washington leads 13–0 entering the 4th quarter, but Pittsburgh closes the gap to 13–7 on a Ray Mathews to Lynn Chandnois lateral run for a touchdown. Defensive halfback Jack Butler becomes just the seventh man in league history to intercept 4 passes in a game (he returns them 86 yards and his longest return of 36 yards has never been accurately credited). When Eddie LeBaron throws a quick out to Charlie Justice from his own end zone (the Skins had just made a goal line stand), Butler reads the route, intercepts, and scores the winning touchdown to keep the Skins out of second place.

1958 The 2–8–1 Cardinals are visiting Forbes Field to face the red-hot 6–4–1 Steelers. Pittsburgh gains 683 yards in total offense (a team record) in defeating Chicago, 38–21. Pro Bowl halfback Tom Tracy goes on to set a season rushing record with 714 yards, yet today he serves his team better as a receiver (106 yards on 7 catches) and passer with a 72-yard option pass touchdown to rookie Jimmy Orr (team record 205 yards receiving on 6 catches), 1 of 3 touchdown catches for Orr.

Bobby Layne throws for a team record 409 yards on 23 completions, and fullback Tank Younger crunches the Cardinals for 106 yards on the ground. The Steeler defense, led by all-pro's Ernie Stautner and Jack Butler (his 49th and 50th career interceptions), has allowed only 10 offensive touchdowns in the last seven games (six wins and a tie).

14

1952 The Rams, after a 1–3 start, have won seven straight games to position themselves for a possible play-off berth. The 5–6 Steelers have designs on being the "spoiler," as they have won two straight by a combined score of 87–14.

Rookie right corner Richard "Night Train" Lane intercepts Ray Mathews's halfback option pass on 3rd and 20 on their own 38-yard line in the 1st quarter. It is just before the half, and the Rams lead 7–0, when Jim Finks on a 2nd and 10 from his own 40 throws toward the sideline, and Lane purloins the pass and gallops 42 yards for a touchdown. Behind 14–7 in the 3rd quarter, Finks, on a 1st and 10 play on the Ram 21, throws downfield, where Lane intercepts on the Ram 8-yard line, setting a new record of 14 interceptions (all in the last nine games) in a season (which still stands 57 years later).

Future Hall of Famer Norm Van Brocklin completes a 65-yard pass to future Hall of Famer Elroy Hirsch, who "crazylegs" his way for the score, and now the Rams lead 21–7. The Rams earn their play-off berth in the 28–14 victory, as they gain 516 yards in total offense (Elroy Hirsch and Tom Fears combine for 230 yards receiving on 14 catches and 3 touchdowns).

1980 The 5–9 Cardinals are at the Vet in Philadelphia to take on a high-flying Eagle team that has won 31 of their last 44 regular-season games. Scoreless at the half, the top-ranked NFC defense, led by Pro Bowl noseguard Charlie Johnson, limits the Cardinals to just 126 yards in total offense for the game (Philadelphia allows just 83 yards a game rushing when they win). When Jim Hart is knocked out of the game, he is replaced by Mike Loyd, who completes just 4 of 15 passing for 44 yards. Philadelphia scores late to clinch the victory, 17–3. The Dick Vermeil rebuilding job is now just one step away.

15

1935   The Lions and Giants are squaring off at University of Detroit Stadium for the league title. Detroit caught fire during the last seven weeks of the season with a 5–1–1 record with a talented and deep roster (especially in the backfield). The Lions drive 61 yards in the 1st quarter, as Ace Gutowsky scores from the 2-yard line. Frank Christiansen intercepts New York back Ed Danowski's pass and returns 30 yards to the Giant 46. On 3rd and 6, future Hall of Famer Earl "Dutch" Clark reverses his field and gallops 40 yards for a touchdown.

The Detroit goal line stand proves to be key just before the half and enables the Lions to keep the lead, 13–7. During the 2nd half, the Lion ground game continues to growl, as Detroit gains 235 yards rushing for the game. Ernie Caddel and Buddy Parker both score on running plays in the 4th quarter as Detroit wins their first championship, 26–7.

1963   The 4–8–1 Vikings are journeying to Franklin Field to play the 2–9–2 Eagles. Philadelphia has the ball 1st and 10 on their own 46-yard line in the 2nd quarter, when Sonny Jurgensen fumbles. Left defensive end Don Hultz recovers the fumble to set a new league record (which still stands) of recovering 9 opponent fumbles in a season. Leading 20–13 in the 4th quarter, Hultz returns an interception 35 yards for a touchdown as the Vikings win, 34–13.

1973   The 6–6–1 Lions are in the Orange Bowl to take on the 11–2 defending Super Bowl champion Dolphins. Paul Warfield has caught 100 passes for 2,187 yards and 25 touchdowns in Miami's 45 victories since 1970. In the games Miami did not win, he caught 23 passes for 539 yards and just 2 touchdowns. Today he continues to shine brightly, as the future Hall of Famer catches 6 pass for 103 yards in the game, yet what really stands out is the fact that Warfield, on a variety of patterns, catches 4 touchdown passes in the 1st half in a 34–7 victory.

16

1951 Entering the 1951 season the Redskins had recorded just four individual 100-yard rushing performances in their last 52 games. Rob Goode sets two records today, as he blasts for 107 yards on 22 carries on a snow-blanketed field in a 20–10 loss to Pittsburgh. Goode has now rushed for more than 100 yards seven times during the season (a new record) and five consecutive (also a new record), as he finishes second in the league in rushing with 951 yards.

1956 The 3–8 Rams are hosting the 4–7 Packers in the Coliseum on a record-setting day for rookie Tommy Wilson of the Rams, as he gains 223 yards (primarily on sweeps and counters) on 23 carries. Tied at 7 in the 1st quarter, Ram right safety Will Sherman intercepts a slant pass to Gary Knafelc and dashes 95 yards for the go-ahead touchdown in a 49–21 Ram victory.

When a team has an individual rush for 100 yards and a teammate returns an interception for a touchdown, that team wins 92 percent of the time. The author's term for this is "apocalyptic horsemen." The Rams have accomplished this feat 34 times (more than any team) and won 32 (94.11 percent).

1962 The 3–9–1 Eagles are taking on the 3–9–1 Cardinals in an air battle in St. Louis. The 1,087 combined total yards (Eagles 498 and Cardinals 589) in the game remains a Cardinal record. Sonny Jurgensen completes 15 of 34 for 419 yards (Tommy McDonald and Timmy Brown combine for 361 yards on 9 catches and all 5 touchdowns). Charley Johnson completes 17 of 32 for 386 yards (a new Cardinal yardage record). The total yards passing (834) is also a new Cardinal record.

Two versatile backs also contribute to the highlights of this game, as John David Crow scores 4 touchdowns (he gains 95 yards rushing and completes 2 option passes for 29 yards), including the winning touchdown in 45–35 Cardinal victory. Brown sets a new record for net yards gained in a season with 2,306 (he gained 341 in this game).

1979 Archie Manning completes 10 of 15 passes for 162 yards and a touchdown in a 29–14 Saint win over the Rams.

2001 Peyton Manning completes 23 of 35 for 325 yards and 3 touchdowns in a 41–27 Colt victory over Atlanta.

2007 Eli Manning completes 18 of 52 for 184 yards and a touchdown in a 22–10 Giant loss to Washington, thus the Manning touchdown pass day in league history.

17

1933 The Giants are invading Wrigley Field for the championship of the league, which is now divided into two divisions. Behind 6–0 in the 2nd quarter, New York's Harry Newman (12 of 17 for 201 yards passing) completes a 29-yard touchdown pass to Red Badgro to get the lead. Trailing 16–14 in the 4th quarter, Newman throws on every down in a drive that culminates in an 8-yard pass to future Hall of Famer Ken Strong.

Chicago gains 63 yards on just 2 pass plays to win the game. Keith Molesworth completes to Carl Brumbaugh for 31 yards to the New York 32-yard line. Future Hall of Fame fullback Bronko Nagurski (who has rushed for 65 yards) lofts a pass to Bill Hewitt for 13 yards, who then laterals to Bill Karr in the flat. Karr dashes up the sideline 19 yards for the winning score in the Bears 23–21 victory.

1944 The Packers, on the road for the sixth consecutive week, are at the Polo Grounds to take on the best defense in the league, led by interception champion Howie Livingston. New York has allowed just 8 offensive touchdowns all season (and has led in pass defense efficiency [24.0]). New York faces the incomparable Don Hutson, who has caught 48 passes for 625 yards and 10 touchdowns in 8 Packer wins. Bill Paschal (the league rushing champion) of the Giants faces a defense that has allowed just 77 yards a game rushing in their eight victories.

Green Bay drives 49 yards on just six plays to take a 7–0 2nd-quarter lead, as Joe "Tiger" Laws and Ted Fritsch break off runs of 21 and 27 yards, respectively, to highlight the drive. Fritsch powers over a determined New York line on 4th down for the score. At 3rd and 7 in the 3rd quarter, Irv Comp fires to Hutson for 24 yards to the New York 30-yard line. Then at 3rd down and 8 on the New York 28, Comp (who completes just 3 of 10 in the game) uses the "Hutson special" and lofts a pass deep up the left sideline to a wide-open Fritsch for the 28-yard touchdown in the 14–7 Packer victory. New York gains 188 yards in total offense in the 2nd half (only 27 yards in the 1st half) but scores only once, as Joe Laws's two 2nd-half interceptions stop drives.

1984 The 9–6 Cowboys are in Miami to take on the 13–2 Dolphins. Dan Marino completes 23 of 40 passes for 340 yards (for a league record of 5,084 yards) for 4 touchdowns (for a league record of 48 in a season) in a 28–21 victory.

18

1949 We are in the Coliseum to watch the Rams face the defending league champion Eagles. Tommy Thompson finds Pete Pihos for a 31-yard 2nd-quarter touchdown and a 7–0 halftime lead. Rookie Leo Skladany blocks and returns a Ram punt 2 yards for the only other score in the 3rd quarter. Future Hall of Famer and league rushing champion Steve Van Buren sets championship game records by toting the ball 31 times for 196 yards. The Philadelphia Eagles are leading the league in pass defense efficiency with a mark of 30.0, and today the vaunted Ram passing attack completes only 10 of 27 for 98 yards as the Eagles record their second consecutive shutout championship victory, final score Philadelphia 14, Rams 0.

1977 Trailing 24–10 in the 3rd quarter at home, the Colts rally to a 30–24 division-title-clinching victory over the Patriots. The excellent Colt secondary led by league-leading interceptor Lyle Blackwood limits Steve Grogan to 11 of 25 passing for 129 yards. Down 24–23 with 8:50 left in the 4th quarter, the Colts drive 99 yards for the winning score behind Bert Jones's passing (19 of 30 for 340 yards).

1983 The 8–7 Patriots are traveling to the Kingdome to play the 8–7 Seahawks for the final wild card berth in the play-offs. Dave Krieg hits future Hall of Famer Steve Largent (7 catches for 133 yards) with a 46-yard touchdown pass in the 2nd quarter to give Seattle a 10–0 lead. Running back Curt Warner pounds out 116 yards on 26 carries in the "ground chuck" offense of Seattle. Warner gains a conference-leading 1,449 yards rushing, but more importantly Seattle goes on to win all six times Warner goes over the 100-yard mark during the season.

Seattle runners produced just nine individual rushing performances of 100 yards or more in the franchise's first 101 games going into this season. Chuck Knox thus becomes the first coach in league history to guide three different teams into the play-offs with this 24–6 victory.

19

1949 The defending league champion Cardinals are in Shibe Park in Philadelphia for the championship rematch with the Eagles. The Al Wistert–led offensive line continually opens holes for Steve Van Buren (98 yards on 26 carries), Bosh Pritchard (67 yards on 16 carries), and quarterback Tommy Thompson (50 yards on 11 carries). Early in the 4th quarter, Van Buren scores from the 5-yard line (after a Bucko Kilroy fumble recovery) in the 7–0 victory as Philadelphia wins their first-ever championship.

1971 The 6–7 Chargers are invading the Astrodome to take on the Oilers. Houston has won just 9 of their last 37 regular-season games and trails 23–7 at the half. Future Hall of Famer Ken Houston returns successive passes by John Hadl for touchdowns (35 and 29 yards) to put the

Oilers ahead for the first time in the game, 35–30. Houston is the first player in league history to return 4 interceptions for a touchdown in a season. He also now holds the record for most interceptions returned for a touchdown in a career with 9 (he accomplishes this in just five seasons).

Late in the 4th quarter, Bob Atkins returns an errant San Diego pass 25 yards for a touchdown as Houston ties a league record by returning 3 interceptions for a touchdown in a game. The 49 points the Oilers score in this game is the most they have scored since October of 1962.

1976 The defending AFC Eastern champion Colts are hosting the Steelers in this divisional round play-off game. Baltimore leads the NFL in total offense with an average of 374 yards a game. Today, however, the legendary "Steel Curtain" defense of Pittsburgh is forged in steel as Baltimore gains just 170 yards in total offense in the 40–14 victory (Pittsburgh has now allowed only 41 points in their last ten games). Quarterback Bert Jones of the Colts gains just 144 yards on his 11 completions (he attempts 25 passes) and is intercepted by safeties Mike Wagner and Glen Edwards. Jones is sacked 5 times, and the Colt run game gains just 71 yards for the game. Future Hall of Famers Terry Bradshaw (14 of 18 for 264 yards) and Franco Harris (132 yards on 18 carries) provide the offense for Pittsburgh as they continue in their quest to become the first team to win three consecutive Super Bowl titles.

20

1970 The 2–11 Patriots are at Riverfront Stadium to take on the 7–6 Bengals. Cincinnati scores the most points in team history (at this point in time) in a 45–7 victory as the

Bengals win the AFC Central Division title. Cincinnati scores on all 6 possessions in the 1st half and defensively allows the fewest yards in team history (at this point in team history) with just 149. Joe Kapp of the Patriots throws the final touchdown pass of his brief career in the NFL.

The 6–7 Packers are at Tiger Stadium to play the 9–4 Lions. During the season, Detroit allowed only 67 yards rushing a game in their ten wins (today Green Bay gains just 46), as they lead the league in this important category. The outstanding cornerback duo of Lem Barney and Dick LeBeau both intercept in this 20–0 victory (the only time in Lion history that they shut out Green Bay twice in a season). Detroit has now won five consecutive games to earn a wild card berth in the play-offs.

1975 The 11–2 defending NFC conference champion Vikings are in Orchard Park to battle the snow and the 8–5 Buffalo Bills. Fran Tarkenton throws 2 touchdown passes to Chuck Foreman as he surpasses John Unitas as the lifetime leader with 291. Foreman, who gains 172 yards rushing and receiving in the game, scores 3 times to tie Gale Sayers's record of 22 touchdowns in a season in the 35–13 victory. O. J. Simpson of the Bills scores twice to establish a new record of 23 touchdowns in a season.

1987 The 8–5 defending AFC Central Browns are at the Coliseum to take on the 5–8 Raiders. Quarterback Bernie Kosar of Cleveland completes 21 of 32 for 294 yards and 2 touchdowns in a 24–17 victory. Kosar goes on to lead the AFC in passing efficiency with a mark of 95.4, as Cleveland again continues on to win the Central Division title.

21

1969   The 12–1 defending NFC Central Division champion Vikings are in Atlanta to battle the 5–8 Falcons. The only touchdown in the Falcon 10–3 victory is scored by left defensive end Claude Humphrey on a 24-yard fumble return. Minnesota allows only 2,720 yards in total offense during the season (194 yards a game). Upon closer inspection, however, during the last seven weeks of the season, Viking opponents gain just 385 yards rushing on 152 attempts (2.53 a carry). The "Purple Gang" goes on to permit just 9 offensive touchdowns in Minnesota's last 13 games. The Vikings head home to battle the Rams in the Western Conference play-offs.

1975   The 10–3 defending NFC Eastern Division champion Cardinals are in the Silverdome to play the 7–6 Lions. Future Hall of Fame offensive lineman Dan Dierdorf leads a Cardinal offensive line that allows only 8 sacks all season and opens holes for a versatile running game.

Jim Otis goes on to lead the NFC in rushing with 1,076 yards (just the second Cardinal to rush for more than 1,000 yards in a season), and today he and outside threat Terry Metcalf combine to gain 107 yards on 23 carries. Jerry Latin comes off the bench to gain 112 yards rushing on just 15 carries (including a 57-yard 3rd-quarter touchdown run) to enable St. Louis to defeat Detroit, 24–13. St. Louis has now won back-to-back Eastern Division titles.

1980   The 10–5 Browns are in Riverfront Stadium to battle the 6–9 Bengals. Brian Sipe completes 24 of 44 passes for 308 yards and 3 touchdowns in a 27–24 victory to win the AFC Central Division title. Behind 17–10 in the 3rd quarter, Sipe throws touchdown passes of 35 and 34 yards to Ricky Feacher to claim the lead for the first time in the game. Sipe again rallies the Browns as Don Cockroft kicks a 22-yard game-winning field goal with 1:35 left in the game. Sipe becomes just the third different quarterback to throw for more than 4,000 yards in a season. In their 11 wins during the season, Sipe completed 248 of 387 for 3,125 yards and 23 touchdowns (with just 7 interceptions).

22

1957   The San Francisco 49ers are playing their first-ever play-off game since joining the NFL, while the Lions have played in three consecutive title game clashes earlier in the decade. The 49ers have won 9 of 16 regular-season encounters with Detroit, but can they finally make it to the title game?

The 60,118 fans at Kezar Stadium have plenty to cheer about in the 1st half as the 49ers build a 24–7 lead. San Francisco's first score came on the "alley oop" for 34 yards, Y. A. Tittle to R. C. Owens (after a fumble recovery by Bill Herchman). Hugh "The King" McElhenny catches Tittle's 47-yard pass for the second score. San Francisco drives 88 yards on 21 plays to score on a 12-yard Tittle to Billy Wilson pass (Wilson goes on to catch 9 for 107 in the game) in response to an earlier Lion touchdown. Tittle completes 12 of 19 in the 1st half for 186 yards and the 3 above-mentioned touchdowns.

Lion pride? McElhenny, behind superb open-field blocking, sweeps right, cuts back, and weaves 71 yards to set up the last 49er score (a Gordy Soltau field goal). The key play of the 3rd quarter is a Bob Long fumble recovery of a Tittle fumble at the 49er 27. Tom Tracy and Gene Gedman of the Lions score on 3 touchdown runs to put Detroit in the lead for the first time, 28–27, early in the 4th quarter (the largest comeback in play-off history). The 49ers have 14 minutes to respond, but the Joe Schmidt–led defense repeatedly blunts Tittle's efforts (Schmidt's interception return sets up Jim Martin's field goal). The Lions continue on to again face Cleveland in the title game.

1963 The 6–7 defending Eastern Division champion Oilers are traveling to Oakland to face the Al Davis–coached 9–4 Raiders. For the first time in AFL history, teams combine for more than 1,000 yards in total offense, as multiple records are set. Quarterbacks George Blanda of Houston and Tom Flores of Oakland combine to throw 11 touchdown passes (an AFL record), while Art Powell gains the second most yards receiving in a game with 247. During the 2nd quarter, both teams combine to score 49 points (also an AFL record). Oakland trails 49–42 entering the 4th quarter but again rallies to win 52–49 (the most points ever scored in an AFL game) to complete the Raider revitalization.

23

1951 The defending league champion Browns are in the Coliseum to play the Rams in a rematch of last years' epic title game clash. Otto Graham's passing (he gains 280 yards passing on 19 completions in the game) has Cleveland ahead 10–7 in the 3rd quarter, but when left defensive end Larry Brink sacks Graham and forces a fumble (Andy Robustelli returns the fumble to the Browns 2-yard line), the Rams are back in the game (the Los Angeles blitz registers 5 sacks and forces 3 interceptions in the game).

The Browns, trailing 17–10 in the 4th quarter, drive 70

yards on 10 plays to tie the game on Ken Carpenter's 5-yard run. Norm Van Brocklin enters the game and on 3rd down and 3 to go at his own 27-yard line fires to split end Tom Fears up the left sideline (he pump fakes to Elroy Hirsch first) for 73 yards and the winning touchdown between two defenders (Elroy Hirsch and Tom Fears combine for 212 yards receiving).

1962   The Dallas Texans are in Houston at Jeppesen Stadium taking on the defending league champion Oilers. Hank Stram takes record-setting touchdown maker Abner Haynes (19) and moves him to flanker (Haynes gains 1,049 yards rushing). The result is a 28-yard touchdown pass from passer rating champion Len Dawson (98.3) and a 2nd-quarter 10–0 lead. George Blanda drives the Oilers goalward, but linebacker E. J. Holub intercepts and returns the ball 43 yards.

Dallas parlays the return into another Haynes touchdown and a 17–0 halftime lead. The champions respond, as Blanda finds Willard Dewveall twice for 51 yards on the scoring drive. Houston's pass rush (6 sacks in the game) stops Dallas, and the Oilers keep attacking until with 5:58 to play Charlie Tolar (1,012 yards gained rushing in the season) punches it in from the 1-yard line to tie the game. A short punt by Dallas, and Blanda is set to win it, but it is blocked by all-AFL linebacker Sherrill Headrick, and we go to overtime.

All-decade safety Johnny Robinson intercepts Blanda in the 5th quarter to stop a drive after captain Haynes elects to "kick to the clock." Left defensive end Bill Hull drops into the flat and intercepts Blanda (he throws 5 picks). The Stram offensive strategy of power running with fullbacks Jack Spikes and rookie Curtis McClinton pays dividends

(147 yards on 35 combined carries) as Dallas moves steadily, and finally at 2:54 of the 6th period Tommy Brooker kicks the winning 25-yard field goal.

24

1950   Bob Waterfield led the Cleveland Rams to a title as a rookie in 1945. Can he lead the Los Angeles Rams to the title against the Browns? The Rams have the most efficient pass offense in the league (80.7), while the Browns have the most efficient pass defense (28.7). Waterfield completes 18 of 31 for 312 yards as the Rams lead 28–27 late in the 4th quarter in a seesaw battle with true swings of momentum.

Three lost fumbles plague Graham and the Browns early on, but can they respond one last time? Otto Graham completes 22 of 32 for 298 yards, yet just as important is his ability to run, as he gains 99 yards on just 12 carries (the Ram defense is aligned to stop league-leading rusher Marion Motley on the draw/trap play).

Down the field come the Browns, and with 28 seconds left Lou Groza kicks them into the lead, 30–28. Norm Van Brocklin enters the game (a rib injury causes him to not split time with Waterfield) and throws deep on target. For the fifth time in the game, the Browns secondary responds with an interception (Warren Lahr), and Cleveland has another champion, this one named the Browns.

1977   The defending Super Bowl champion Raiders are in Baltimore to play the three-time defending AFC Eastern Division champion Colts. Trailing 10–7 at the half (the only Colt touchdown came on Bruce Laird's interception return), Ken Stabler's play-action 41-yard completion to

Cliff Branch (6 catches for 113 yards) sets up the go-ahead score (Dave Casper).

The lead changes hands five more times before future Hall of Famer Casper makes his famous over-the-head 42-yard catch "ghost to the post" to set up the tying field goal. In overtime (6th quarter), Stabler (345 yards on 21 completions) finds Casper in the end zone for the winning score.

1995   The 8–7 Dolphins are traveling to St. Louis to play the 7–8 Rams in Don Shula's last regular-season game as a coach. Leading 27–22 in the 4th quarter, Dan Marino (290 yards on 23 completions) takes Miami on a long scoring drive to cement the 41–22 victory for the play-off-bound Dolphins. Thus, Don Shula wins more regular-season games, with 328, than any other coach in history.

25

1971   There are thousands of games in pro football history, yet this one game ranks as one of the truly memorable battles. How so, you ask? Any game that lasts 82 minutes and is tied at the half and the end of the 3rd, 4th, and 5th quarters must be memorable.

The Chiefs jump out to a 10–0 lead in their last game at Municipal Stadium, as Ed Podolak catches a 7-yard touchdown pass from Len Dawson. The opportunistic Dolphins parlay a fumble recovery into a field goal with just 16 seconds left in the half to tie the game at 10.

We have 2 Hall of Fame coaches and 11 Hall of Fame players, yet Pro Bowl running back Ed Podolak of the Chiefs, in the performance of his career, is the main ingredient in this thriller. The Dolphin defense has chosen to use roll strong coverage to double team Otis Taylor of Kansas

City, thus the use of Podolak on pass patterns out of the backfield (110 yards on 8 catches), and a variety of running plays (85 yards on 17 carries) keys the Chief attack, along with the tough inside running of Wendell Hayes (100 yards rushing). Every time the Chiefs score, the Dolphins respond and tie the game due to Bob Griese's passes to Paul Warfield (140 yards on 7 catches) and the running of Larry Csonka and Jim Kiick (142 yards on 39 carries combined).

In the last minute of regulation, Podolak returns the kickoff 78 yards (155 yards on kick returns) to set up Jan Stenerud's field goal attempt, which he misses. Now in the 6th quarter and Griese with a "roll right trap left" call, Csonka breaks through and rumbles 29 yards to set up Garo Yepremian's 37-yard game-winning field goal for Miami's first-ever play-off victory.

1993   San Francisco is 10–4 and at home (they have won 18 of their last 19 home games) to take on the 10–4 Oilers. Houston has allowed just 13 offensive touchdowns and an average of just 69 yards a game rushing in a nine-game win streak. Though Warren Moon (195 of 323 for 2,196 yards with 15 touchdowns and only 7 interceptions) has been accurate in the "run and shoot" during the streak. The Oilers have also been averaging 133 yards a game on the ground (Gary Brown gains 114 rushing in this game). Houston continues on their win streak, as they grind out a 10–7 victory over San Francisco.

26

1954 and 1955   We are witnessing the only time in league history that a team wins a championship on the same calendar date a year apart. The Cleveland Browns dominate the Lions and Rams, 89–24. Otto Graham runs for 5 touchdowns in the two title game victories, yet it is his accurate passing that is the difference. Graham completes 23 of 37 for 372 yards and 5 touchdowns (he is sacked just once behind the airtight pass pocket provided by the Brown offense line).

Every game has its key plays, and these two games are no exception. The Browns are aligned in a tight "T" formation with a full house backfield in the 2nd quarter with a 28–10 lead. Graham sends left halfback Ray Renfro on a seam streak past the Lions secondary (both tight ends ran crossing routes to occupy the safeties), and Renfro makes a fingertip catch for 31 yards and a touchdown.

The Rams trail 3–0 in 2nd quarter of the 1955 title game, when Norm Van Brocklin throws to Volney Quinlan on a "hitch" route, which is deflected by right corner Don Paul. Paul intercepts the deflection and scampers 65 yards for the 1st Brown touchdown.

Cleveland deploys defensemen in multiple alignments in both games, and both the Lions and Rams force passes into the teeth of the coverage. In the two games, the Browns record an incredible 13 interceptions (out of 72 passes attempted) for 225 yards in returns. Left safety Ken Konz is the main culprit, with 4 interceptions. Future Hall of Famer Otto Graham retires a champion.

1982 The 2–5 Bears are in Anaheim Stadium to play the 1–6 Rams. Walter Payton becomes the fourth man in league history to gain more than 10,000 yards rushing as he gains 104 in the game (he also catches 5 passes for 102 yards) for a 34–26 victory. Vince Ferragamo passes for 509 yards (he is only the third man in history to accomplish this feat) on 30 completions, but interceptions by Bear safeties

Gary Fencik and Jeff Fisher in the 1st half help Chicago to a 20–16 lead.

2004 The 11–3 Colts are hosting the 11–3 Chargers in a game Peyton Manning will long remember. His 21-yard touchdown pass to Brandon Stokely with less than a minute left in regulation sets a new record for touchdown passes in a season, with 49, and ties the game. The Colts win in overtime, 34–31. Manning completes 27 of 44 for 383 yards in the matchup.

27

1964 The 12–2 Colts are at Municipal Stadium to play the 10–3–1 Browns for the title. Baltimore leads the league in offense with an average of 341 yards per game, while the Browns are ranked third in the league with an average of 320 yards per game. The cold, windy conditions and excellent defensive play by both teams result in an unexpected 0–0 tie at the half. Hall of Famer Lou Groza kicks a 43-yard field goal early in the 3rd quarter to break the deadlock.

Now, on their 2nd possession of the 2nd half, Cleveland is aligned in a double wing set, and here comes fullback Jim Brown on a toss sweep to the left. Behind crisp, determined blocking, Brown is loose in the secondary and cuts to the right, and 46 yards later the Browns are on the Colt 18. Pro Bowl quarterback Frank Ryan fires just under the crossbar to Gary Collins for the 1st of 3 touchdowns.

John Unitas completes just 6 passes for 71 yards to his trio of excellent receivers (Raymond Berry, Jimmy Orr, and John Mackey), as the Cleveland secondary plays tight man-to-man coverage. Jim Brown rumbles for 114 yards rushing, and Frank Ryan completes 5 passes to Collins for 130 yards, usually when Baltimore was in roll weak coverage to Pro Bowl split end Paul Warfield's side of the field. Collins becomes the first receiver in play-off history to catch 3 touchdown passes, as the Browns win, 27–0.

1975 The 11–3 Cardinals are in the Coliseum to play the 12–2 Rams. Though Cardinal quarterback Jim Hart gains 291 yards passing, 2 of the 3 interceptions he throws are disastrous (Jack Youngblood 47-yard and Bill Simpson 65-yard touchdown returns) in the 35–23 Ram victory. In the past three years, Lawrence McCutcheon has gained 2,686 yards rushing (555 carries) in Ram victories, Today, however, is his record-setting day as he gains 202 yards rushing on 37 carries in the Chuck Knox offense.

1981 The 10–6 Bills are at Shea Stadium to battle the 10–5–1 Jets in the wild card round of the play-offs. Buffalo builds a 31–13 4th-quarter lead before the Jets rally behind Richard Todd's passing (377 yards) to close the gap to 31–27 and have the ball with less than a minute left. Safety Bill Simpson of Buffalo intercepts to preserve the victory (he now has a record 9 play-off interceptions).

28

1947 The 9–4 Eagles are in Comiskey Park to take on the 8–4 Cardinals. League rushing champion Steve Van Buren (1,008 yards) is limited to 26 yards on 18 carries, yet Tommy Thompson sets a championship game record for completions (27) to keep Philadelphia in the game. Cardinal halfback Elmer Angsman twice scores on 70-yard explosions through the Eagle defense (159 yards rushing on

10 carries). Chicago leads 14–7 in the 3rd quarter, when Joe Muha punts to Charlie Trippi, and away he goes across the frozen turf (he even slips at the Eagle 30) to scamper 75 yards for a touchdown (Trippi also scores in the 1st quarter on a 44-yard run) as the Cardinals win their only championship, 28–21.

1958 The Colts are in their first championship game, while the veteran Giants are just two years removed from winning the title. New York draws first blood on Pat Summerall's 36-yard field goal, but the Colts respond with a 20-yard drive (after recovering a Frank Gifford fumble) to score on Alan Ameche's 1-yard run. Baltimore drives 86 yards on 15 plays culminating in a John Unitas to Raymond Berry 14-yard touchdown pass.

Vince Lombardi, in his last game as a Giant assistant coach, directs Charlie Conerly to pass (10 of 14 for 187 yards) into the middle zone of the Colt secondary. New York scores twice to take a 4th-quarter 17–14 lead.

Baltimore's defense has overcome the loss of middle linebacker Leo Sanford, as reserve Steve Myhra plays right outside linebacker and Don Shinnick moves to the middle. New York gains just 88 yards rushing on 31 carries the entire game (Gifford's 38-yard run is the only time the Giants outflank the Colts).

Johnny U., in a masterful job of play calling and passing, drives the Colts 86 yards for the tying field goal against Tom Landry's defense (even using "nickle" coverage at times). Three times for 62 yards on the drive Berry makes key receptions.

Though the Giants have the ball first in overtime, they cannot sustain a drive and punt, and here comes Unitas and the Colts again. An Ameche draw play for 23 yards positions the Colts to kick the winning field goal, but not Johnny U., who does not "place much strength in field goals." Out of a wing set Ameche drives over right tackle, and the Colts are champions, 23–17.

29

1963 The 11–3 New York Giants are traveling to Wrigley Field to battle the 11–1–2 Bears for the championship (the fifth time they have met to decide the league title). Y. A. Tittle has broken his own record of touchdown passes in a season with 36 and is the most efficient passer in the league with a rating of 104.8.

The George Allen–coached defense of the Bears has allowed just 97 yards a game rushing and 11 offensive touchdowns in their 11 wins. They rank first in pass defense efficiency with a rating of 34.8 (and have intercepted 36 passes). Though the Giants score first (Y. A. Tittle to Frank Gifford for 14 yards), the Bears continually intercept Tittle (5 times). Chicago twice capitalizes on field position and scores twice on Bill Wade sneaks in the 14–10 victory.

1968 The 13–2 defending AFL champion Raiders are in Shea Stadium to battle the 11–3 Jets. Oakland averaged 172 yards a game rushing in their 12 regular-season victories, while the Jets allowed only 78 yards rushing and 17 offensive touchdowns in their 11 wins. George Sauer and Don Maynard combined for 2,438 yards for New York, but the Raiders are the most efficient pass defense in the AFL (44.8).

New York's defense allows the Raiders just 50 yards rushing in the game, but Daryle Lamonica responds by passing for 401 yards to finally get the Raiders the lead,

23–20, in the 4th quarter. Future Hall of Famer Joe Namath finds Maynard (118 yards on 6 catches) on a deep fade route up the right sideline to set up the winning 6-yard pass, as New York advances to the Super Bowl, 27–23.

1974   The Steelers and Raiders are meeting for the third consecutive season in the play-offs. Pittsburgh ranks first in pass defense efficiency (44.8) and has allowed just 11 offensive touchdowns in their ten wins. Although Ken Stabler throws for 271 yards on his 19 completions, left linebacker Jack Ham of the Steelers "picks" him twice, while the "Steel Curtain" allows the Raiders just 29 yards rushing. Franco Harris and Rocky Bleier grind out 209 yards rushing (47 carries), as Pittsburgh scores twenty-one 4th-quarter points in a 24–13 victory to advance to their first Super Bowl.

30

1956   The Bears and Giants tied in their regular-season game in November, and now the league title is at stake in the rematch in Yankee Stadium. The Tom Landry–coached Giant defense allowed 215 yards per game when they lost but only 85 when they did not. Chicago, with league rushing champion Rick Casares leading the way, averaged 249 yards a game rushing when they won, yet only 93 when they did not.

The Bears gain just 67 yards rushing on 32 carries against the defense led by Andy Robustelli and Sam Huff. The Chicago passing game gains 192 yards but cannot score in the air. The Vince Lombardi–coached offense successfully mixes the run (126 yards) and the pass (222 yards) in a 47–7 victory. Halfbacks Frank Gifford and Alex

Webster combine to catch 9 passes for 207 yards to key the attack.

1973   Due to the league's rotational basis, the 13–2 Vikings are in Dallas to play the 11–4 Cowboys in the NFC Championship Game. The Dallas running game averaged 173 yards a game in the regular season, while the Viking running game averaged 176 when they won (only 81 when they lost). So which defense, "Doomsday" or "Purple Gang," lives up to their nickname in stopping these excellent ground attacks?

Minnesota continually blocks the flex defense as the Vikings gain 203 yards rushing, while Robert Newhouse and Walt Garrison muster just 49 yards on 19 carries for the Cowboys. Right corner Bobby Bryant salts the game away for the Vikings when he returns a Roger Staubach pass 63 yards for a touchdown in the 4th quarter, as Minnesota wins, 27–10.

1984   The 10–6 Bears are in Washington to battle the 11–5 defending NFC champion Redskins. Future Hall of Famer Walter Payton gains 104 yards rushing to propel the Chicago offense, yet it is his 19-yard option pass to tight end Pat Dunsmore on a crossing route for a touchdown after faking a reverse that is the key play in the game, as the Bears lead 10–3 at the half. Led by Pro Bowlers Todd Bell, Richard Dent, Mike Singletary, and Dan Hampton, the Bears stuff John Riggins (50 yards on 21 carries) and record 7 sacks in the 23–19 victory. For the first time in 21 years, the Bears win a play-off game.

31

1961   The 10–3–1 New York Giants are at City Stadium in Green Bay to battle the 11–3 Packers for the league title.

Paul Hornung has led the league in scoring for the third consecutive year, and today he scores 19 points in the 37–0 Packer victory.

Green Bay gains 345 yards in total offense, paced by Hornung's 136 yards rushing and receiving. Green Bay drives 80 yards on 12 plays to take a 7–0 2nd-quarter lead. The key play on the drive is a 3rd and 6 flare pass (the only completed pass of the drive) to Hornung for 26 yards. On 2nd and goal on the 6, Hornung scores on a trap right.

New York scored 368 points during the season, but today the Packer defense allows the Giants only 130 yards in total offense and takes the ball away from New York 5 times. The Packers are champions for the first time in 17 years.

1972 The defending Super Bowl champion Cowboys are at RFK Stadium to lasso the Redskins. In the 20 regular-season games Washington has won since George Allen became coach, the opposition has completed just 282 passes for 2,709 yards (4.69 a pass) for 12 touchdowns. The ball-hawking Redskin defense has intercepted 38 passes in those 20 victories.

Today, Roger Staubach completes just 9 of 20 passes for 98 yards. Walt Garrison and Calvin Hill combine to gain just 37 yards on 16 carries, as Dallas cannot reach the end zone. Future Hall of Famer Charley Taylor catches 7 passes for 146 yards and 2 touchdowns to key the Redskin offense. League MVP Larry Brown hammers out 88 yards on the ground, as Washington controls the clock and the game. The Redskins dethrone Dallas, 26–3, and Allen goes on to return to Los Angeles for the Super Bowl.

2005 The 10–5 Giants are in Oakland to take on the 4–11 Raiders. Tiki Barber goes on to set a new Giant season record for yards rushing with 1,860, and tonight he goes over the 200-yard barrier for the third time in the season (203 on 28 carries). Barber scores the 1st touchdown of the game on a 95-yard burst up the middle at 8:16 of the 1st quarter, as New York goes on to win the NFC Eastern Division title, 30–21. Barber has now gained 1,357 yards in his last ten games.

January

1

1967 The two-time defending league champion Buffalo Bills are meeting the Kansas City Chiefs at War Memorial Stadium for the right to represent the AFL in the first AFL–NFL Championship. The second-ranked Chief defense rises to the occasion to stop the Bill offense. Buffalo gains just 40 yards rushing and late in the 1st half are driving to tie the game. Jack Kemp's pass is pilfered by free safety Johnny Robinson of the Chiefs, who returns the ball 72 yards to set up Mike Mercer's 32-yard field goal with three seconds left in the half.

With a 17–7 lead, the 2nd half is dominated by the Chiefs, who benefit from multiple formations and precision execution by future Hall of Fame quarterback Len Dawson. Dawson completes 9 passes for 154 yards to the crack receiving combo of Chris Burford and Otis Taylor, while the Kansas City ground attack grinds out 113 yards rushing.

While the Bills pass rush registers 63 yards in sacks, it is not enough, as the Chiefs still score twice. Rookie Mike

Garrett runs for the touchdowns (including a weaving run of 18 yards) in the 31–7 victory.

Hours later in the Cotton Bowl in Dallas, two former New York Giant assistant coaches and future Hall of Famers Vince Lombardi and Tom Landry are matching wits and wills. An excellent trap block right by Fuzzy Thurston on Elijah Pitts's 24-yard run sets up the first Packer touchdown (Bart Starr to Elijah Pitts on a circle route to the right for 17 yards). Don Perkins, on a counterright, scores the 2nd Cowboy touchdown from 23 yards out. Starr looks left and comes back to the right and completes a post to Carroll Dale for 51 yards and touchdown for a 21–17 lead at the half.

Green Bay and Dallas ranked 2–3 in total defense during the regular season, yet it is a game of big plays (Dallas 418 and Green Bay 367) on offense. Starr completes 11 of 18 for 168 yards, while Don Meredith, overcoming a wild streak (7 straight incompletions), completes 8 of 19 for 135 yards in the 2nd half.

Frank Clarke catches passes for 102 yards in the 2nd half (the first Packer opponent to go over the century mark in a play-off game). Don Perkins pounds out 108 yards rushing for Dallas, but it is Starr with 4 key 3rd-down completions in the 2nd half that is the difference in the 34–27 victory.

2

1972 Miami has won their first division title. They are hosting division rival and defending Super Bowl champion Baltimore in the AFC Championship Game. The Colt defense has allowed only 17 offensive touchdowns in 15 games. They rank first in pass defense efficiency (44.2), and Colt opponents average about 80 yards per game rushing. How will the Dolphins move the ball and score on this horseshoe-hard defense?

Bob Griese continues to attempt to attack the Colts on the ground, as Jim Kiick and Larry Csonka gain 129 rushing on 31 attempts. The Dolphin difference maker is future Hall of Fame receiver Paul Warfield, who scores on a 75-yard reception from Griese in the 1st quarter. Although the Colts move the ball into Dolphin territory, they cannot get on the scoreboard, as Jim O'Brien misses 3 field goals and has a 4th blocked.

John Unitas's long pass in the 3rd quarter is tipped by right corner Curtis Johnson and pilfered by Dick Anderson, who weaves his way 62 yards for a touchdown behind a wall of open field cut blocks. Griese completes just 4 of 8, but his 50-yard strike to Warfield in the 4th quarter sets up Csonka's 5-yard touchdown run. Baltimore is shut out for the first time in 97 games, and Don Shula's Dolphins are headed to their first Super Bowl.

1982 Ten years later to the day and Miami is again at home to face the league-leading San Diego offense (421 yards per game). The Orange Bowl crowd is stunned as the Chargers bolt out to a 24–0 1st-quarter lead under the stewardship of Dan Fouts. Miami, under relief pitcher Don Strock, roars back with 17 unanswered points, including a "hook and ladder" pass play just before the half.

The Dolphins forge ahead 38–31 as Strock throws for 397 yards. Charger defenders Linden King and Gary Johnson force an Andra Franklin fumble. Fouts is fabulous in driving the Chargers 82 yards on 10 plays for the tying score. With less than a minute left in regulation, Miami drives into San Diego territory, but Uwe Von Schamann's field goal attempt is blocked by Kellen Winslow. San Diego breaks 15 divisional team play-off records. Winslow's near-mythical performance, with 13 receptions for 166 yards, is the highlight in the 41–38 overtime victory.

3

1971 It is the first year of the merger, and championship Sunday takes us to Kezar Stadium in San Francisco. For the first time in team history, the 49ers had won a play-off game and are now hosting the Dallas Cowboys; the winner goes to the Super Bowl. Bruce Gossett kicks a 16-yard field goal to put the 49ers ahead 3–0 at the end of the 1st quarter.

The Cowboys set team play-off records for rushing attempts (51) and 1st downs (16). Rookie Duane Thomas carries the ball 27 times for a record 143 yards (a record that lasts nine years). Thomas's 13-yard touchdown run in the 3rd quarter puts Dallas ahead for the first time in the game, and they do not surrender the lead.

Later in the 3rd quarter, quarterback Craig Morton flips 5 yards to fullback Walt Garrison for a touchdown to put Dallas ahead, 17–3. Now in his 14th season, quarterback John Brodie leads San Francisco back down the field on an 8-play 73-yard drive to narrow the margin to 17–10 on a 26-yard touchdown pass to Dick Witcher. The Dallas flex defense keeps the lead and, for the first time, the Cowboys are going to the Super Bowl.

Early in the 1st quarter, left defensive end Bubba Smith of the Colts sacks and smashes Raider quarterback Daryle Lamonica to the ground. Entering the game at the age of 43, as he had numerous times during the season, is George Blanda. Blanda completes 17 of 32 passes for 271 yards and 2 touchdowns to keep the Raiders in the game.

During the regular season, the Colts allowed just 102 yards a game rushing and only 6 rushing touchdowns all season. The Raiders gain 107 rushing for the game, while the Colts, under the savvy guidance of 37-year-old John Unitas (11 of 30 for 245 yards), mix the run with pass. The hard-edged Colt defense registers 5 sacks and takes the ball away from Oakland 4 times to keep Baltimore ahead.

John Unitas, with a 20–17 lead in the 4th quarter, saves his best play for when he needs it most. Expecting man coverage by the Raiders, John puts wide receiver Ray Perkins at fullback and runs him out of the backfield on an out-and-up pattern. Behind the Raider defense, Perkins catches the well-thrown Unitas pass for the clinching 68-yard touchdown. On to Miami and the Super Bowl.

4

1976 On opening day 1975, the Dallas Cowboys defeated the Rams, 18–7. The Rams rebounded from this loss to again win the NFC Western Division and an impressive play-off victory over the Cardinals. The Cowboys earned a wild card berth, while finishing second to the Cardinals in the NFC Eastern Division and gaining an impressive road play-off victory over the Vikings ("hail mary").

The 84,483 fans in the Los Angeles Coliseum are in for a shock, as Dallas completely controls the game, 37–7. Future Hall of Fame quarterback Roger Staubach completes 16 of 26 for 220 yards and 4 touchdowns. Running back Preston Pearson scores the 1st Cowboy touchdown on an 18-yard screen pass. Out of the spread ("shotgun") formation, Pearson makes an outstanding diving touchdown reception for 15 yards on an out-and-up pattern from Staubach in the 2nd quarter.

Leading 21–0 in the 3rd quarter, Staubach flips the ball to Pearson on a shovel pass for 19 yards and a touchdown (his record-setting 3rd). The Dallas "Doomsday" defense holds the Rams to just 118 yards in total offense. The Cowboys are headed to Miami and the Super Bowl.

1986 It is ten years to the day, except we are in Anaheim Stadium before 66,351 fans to witness the Rams and Cowboys again in the play-offs (for the eighth time). The excellent Ram 3–4 defense takes the ball away from Dallas 6 times (3 interceptions and 3 fumble recoveries) and records 5 sacks to shut out the Cowboys for the first time in their play-off history.

Quarterback Dieter Brock of the Rams completes only 6 of 22 passes for just 50 yards. Eric Dickerson gains 78 yards rushing in the 1st half, as the Rams led only 3–0. On his 1st carry of the 2nd half, Dickerson explodes for 55 yards and a touchdown. Early in the 4th quarter, Dickerson breaks loose again, this time for 40 yards and a touchdown. He sets the league record of 248 yards rushing (34 attempts) in a play-off game.

The 20–0 victory takes the Rams to Chicago to play a Chicago Bear team they had beaten two consecutive years in the regular season, games in which Dickerson gained a combined 276 yards rushing on 62 carries. Would Dickerson and the Rams be able to continue to run the ball effectively against the best defense in pro football?

5

1964 Eleven games into their season, the Boston Patriots' record stood at 5–5–1. Not exactly championship caliber, but by winning two of their last three games, the Patriots earned a tie for first in the Eastern Division and a play-off game against the Buffalo Bills. Running back Larry Garron (164 yards rushing and receiving) is the difference in the 26–8 victory over Buffalo. The Patriots move on to travel to Balboa Stadium, in San Diego, to take on the Chargers.

Though the Patriots lost twice to San Diego in the regular season, both games had been close defensive struggles (17–13 and 7–6). Boston's blitzing, cohesive defensive team with six AFL all-stars (Bob Dee, Larry Eisenhauer, Houston Antwine, Tom Addison, Nick Buoniconti, and Ron Hall) limited the outstanding running back tandem of Keith Lincoln and Paul Lowe to just 82 yards rushing on 32 attempts in the two games. In fact, Larry Garron outgained the tandem with 157 yards on 42 carries.

Head coach Sid Gillman had coached in three championship games in his career and had lost all of them. This time it would be different. El Sid uses man in motion, quick pitch running plays to the outside and counters to combat the Boston blitz. How effective was Gillman's game play, you ask? San Diego gained 610 yards in total offense.

Early in the 1st quarter, Keith Lincoln rips off a 56-yard run to the Patriot 4-yard line, leading to a Tobin Rote touchdown run. Later in the 1st quarter, Lincoln, on a sweep left burst, goes for 67 yards down the sideline for a touchdown. After Larry Garron scores the only Patriot touchdown on a 7-yard run, it is Paul Lowe's turn to show his stuff. Lowe's smooth-striding 58-yard touchdown run closes the scoring in the 1st quarter.

Boston quarterback Babe Parilli struggles the entire game, as he completes just 14 of 29 for 189 yards. His former Green Bay teammate Tobin Rote mixes his passes judiciously as he completes 10 of 15 for 173 yards and 2 touchdowns. Rote's long, high aerial down the left sideline to future Hall of Famer Lance Alworth for a 48-yard touchdown reception over corner Bob Suci is a sight to behold.

Keith Lincoln sets numerous team and league records, as he gains 329 yards rushing and receiving (on just 20 plays). The powder-blue-clad Chargers go on to earn their first and only AFL title, 51–10.

6

1985   The Dolphins are hosting the AFC title game for the first time in 11 years. Future Hall of Fame quarterback Dan Marino sets an AFC title game record, as well as a Dolphin team record, by passing for 421 yards. His completions average 20 yards, and he continually beats the Steelers blitz and throws vertically down the field.

Pittsburgh stays in the game, as Jon Stallworth again gains more than 100 yards receiving as his team leads 14–10 with just 90 seconds left in the half. Marino hits Mark Duper for 41 yards and a touchdown on a streak pattern. Lyle Blackwood intercepts for the "Killer Bees," and with just 36 seconds left in the half, running back Tony Nathan plunges for 2 yards and a 24–14 lead.

Early in the 3rd quarter, Marino completes deep for 36 yards to Duper and a touchdown. Tony Nathan gains 178 yards rushing and receiving, and Duper finishes with a then team record 148 receiving. Pittsburgh does not go quietly, as they gain 455 yards in total offense before succumbing, 45–28. Amazingly, there are no sacks, although there are 69 passes attempted.

1990   We are at the battle of the Lake Erie warriors, as first-year head coach Bud Carson and his Cleveland

Browns are hosting the Buffalo Bills. Future Hall of Fame quarterback Jim Kelly's ability to allow his receivers to run after the catch enables Buffalo to twice take the lead in the 1st half on touchdown passes to Andre Reed (72 yards) and James Lofton (33 yards).

Bernie Kosar's 11th play-off touchdown pass (a new team record) to Webster Slaughter on a 52-yard streak up the left sideline in the 1st quarter and his 44-yard corner route to Slaughter early in the 3rd quarter have reclaimed the lead from the Bills, 24–14. Thurman Thomas is deployed throughout the game in many different alignments by offensive coordinator Ted Marchibroda, and he responds with 13 receptions for 150 yards. When Thomas catches a short touchdown pass with four minutes left, the Bills pull to 34–30.

Although the Bills gain 453 yards in total offense and drive to the Cleveland 11-yard line late in the game, it is Brown left outside linebacker Clay Matthews who makes the defensive play of the game, as he intercepts the final throw to Thomas. Cleveland goes on to return to the AFC title game for the third time in four years.

7

1979 The defending Super Bowl champion Dallas Cowboys are in the Coliseum to play the Rams in the NFC title game before a crowd of 67,470. Future Hall of Famer Tony Dorsett gained 1,325 yards rushing for the season to help Dallas lead the NFC in this important category. The Cowboys are also the most difficult team to run on, as they allow only 1,721 yards rushing. The Rams, under new defensive coordinator Bud Carson, lead the NFC in pass defense efficiency with a mark of 50.2.

Strong safety Charlie Waters returns a Pat Haden interception to the Ram 10-yard line in the 3rd quarter, setting up the 1st Cowboy touchdown (a Dorsett 5-yard run). Waters returns his next Haden interception to the Ram 20-yard line, lining up a touchdown pass from Roger Staubach to Scott Laidlaw. Ahead by 21 late in the 4th quarter, outside linebacker Thomas "Hollywood" Henderson makes the longest interception return in Cowboy play-off history with a 68–yard touchdown return.

Pittsburgh has set league defensive records for a 16-game schedule (including fewest points allowed with 195). The Houston Oilers have proven they can beat Pittsburgh in Three Rivers Stadium, but can they do it twice?

The Steeler ground game pounds out 172 yards on 44 attempts, and quarterback Terry Bradshaw gains 200 yards on his 11 completions. Though impressive, the difference in this game is the "Steel Curtain," especially one of their future Hall of Famers.

Left linebacker Jack Ham recovers an Earl Campbell fumble at the Oiler 17-yard line to set up Rocky Bleier's 15-yard touchdown run. Ham strips Oiler running back Ronnie Coleman in the open field and then recovers the ball. Terry Bradshaw throws to Lynn Swann for 29 yards and a touchdown on the ensuing drive.

Pittsburgh recovers 2 more fumbles that lead to scores just before the half. League rushing champion Earl Campbell gains just 26 yards on 15 carries in the 1st half as Houston trails, 31–0. Jack Ham sets up a short field goal with his interception (1 of 5 by Pittsburgh), and he also records 1 of the Steelers 4 sacks. During the regular season, the excellent Oiler offensive line permitted only 17.

8

1983 The Packers are back in the play-offs for the first time in ten years to take on the St. Louis Cardinals at Lambeau Field. On the 3rd play of the Packers 2nd possession, quarterback Lynn Dickey hits John Jefferson on a 60-yard touchdown pass to take the lead, 7–3. Dickey completes 17 of 23 for 260 yards (11.30 yards per pass). Ottis Anderson gains 58 yards rushing by early in the 2nd quarter, but a severe ankle injury takes him out of the game and the Cardinal running attack fizzles.

Green Bay scores 3 touchdowns in the 2nd quarter to lead 28–9 at the half. The Packer offensive line keeps Dickey upright the entire game, as he is not sacked, and he continues to find John Jefferson open. Jefferson catches 6 passes for 148 yards in the game, including a 7-yard touchdown reception in the 3rd quarter.

Cardinal quarterback Neil Lomax gains 385 yards passing on his 31 completions. The Packer pass rush gets to Lomax 5 times and takes the ball away 4 times. Although Lomax is able to throw his 2nd touchdown pass (to Mike Schumann) in the 4th quarter, this cosmetic score is not nearly enough as Green Bay advances in the tournament, 41–16.

1994 Eleven years to the day and Green Bay has not won a play-off game. In the final game of the 1993 regular season, the Packers lose the NFC Central Division title to Detroit as Brett Favre throws 4 interceptions. The result is a rematch but this time in the Pontiac Silverdome in Detroit. These two teams had played 121 times in the regular season, yet this is the first-ever play-off meeting of the squads.

Barry Sanders is back in the Detroit lineup, and he gains

169 yards rushing on 27 carries. Wide receiver Brett Perriman catches 10 passes for 150 yards but none in the 4th quarter. Leading 17–14 in the 3rd quarter, Erik Kramer's pass to Ty Hallock in the end zone is intercepted by Packer safety George Teague, who goes 101 yards for a Green Bay touchdown.

Detroit fights back into the lead, 24–21, and now with less than a minute remaining Brett Favre runs to his left and throws back across the field to a wide-open Sterling Sharpe in the Lion end zone for 40 yards and the winning touchdown (Sharpe's 3rd touchdown of the game).

9

1977   Eight years, 87 regular-season victories, and 7 division championships, and we now have the fourth appearance for the Minnesota Vikings in the Super Bowl. This veteran group, led by future Hall of Fame coach Bud Grant, has demonstrated time and again the ability to make the "big play" in regular-season and play-off victories. Was this finally their time?

Since December of 1968, when the Raiders lost to the Jets, the stigma (much like the Vikings) of getting to a championship game and losing was a dark cloud for the silver and black. Nine years later and in their seventh AFC Championship Game, and they finally have a victory (over Pittsburgh). The Raiders won 13 regular-season games in their Super Bowl seasons of 1967 and 1976. Was this finally their time?

Ken "The Snake" Stabler has punctured secondaries all year, as he led the league with 27 touchdown passes, yet a truer indicator of the strength of the Raider passing game is that "The Snake" led the league in touchdown pass percentage per attempt (9.3 percent). This is the highest percentage since Y. A. Tittle of the Giants in 1963 with 9.8 percent.

The Raiders averaged about 40 running plays a game. This offensive balance was a key ingredient in their success. Usually running to the left behind future Hall of Famers Art Shell (tackle) and Gene Upshaw (guard), the punishing Raider ground game gained a record 266 yards on 52 attempts.

Stabler gains 79 yards on 4 completions to the game's MVP Fred Biletnikoff in key situations, and he throws only 19 times the entire game. The Raiders set a Super Bowl record with 429 yards in total offense.

The game is scoreless in the 1st quarter, and Fred McNeil blocks Ray Guy's punt setting up a 1st and goal situation. When Willie Hall recovers a fumble, the Raiders drive 90 yards for a field goal. The next time Oakland gains control of the ball, they push 64 yards for a touchdown and a 10–0 lead. Behind 26–7 with about six minutes left in the game, Fran Tarkenton throws a quick out to his left, and "Old Man Willie" breaks on the ball. Willie Brown's 75-yard interception return is the icing on the cake in the 32–14 victory.

10

1982 The 60,525 fans at Candlestick Park are on their feet. It is 3rd down and 3 yards to go on the Dallas 6-yard line with 58 seconds left in the game, and San Francisco trails by 6 points, yet before we go to the outcome of the game some background is needed.

Going into the 1981 regular season, Bill Walsh had never beaten the Cowboys (0–3), and his teams had been outscored 118 to 37. Before the 1981 season began, the 49ers had won just 10 of their last 51 league games. San Francisco had lost all three of their play-off games to Dallas in the early 1970s.

The year 1981 has been magical for Frisco, with a 13–3 regular-season record (including a victory over the Cowboys), a division championship, and a first-round play-off victory over the New York Giants. They are one victory from the Super Bowl, but the opponent they face is battle tested and very well coached.

The Dallas defense led the league in interceptions with 37. They were one of the two teams that ran the ball for more than 2,700 yards. The Cowboys had lost in the play-offs three straight seasons. They believed it was time for another Super Bowl victory.

As the 49ers began that fateful drive in the 4th quarter, there had already been six lead changes. Dallas struggles to run the ball effectively against the 49er defense but takes the ball away 6 times. Joe Montana had already thrown for more than 200 yards and 2 touchdowns.

Bill Walsh realizes as the drive begins that Tom Landry was going to play "nickle" defense; therefore, Walsh mixes in running plays with Lenvil Elliott and a key reverse with wide receiver Freddie Solomon. Dwight Clark had already caught 7 passes for 114 yards in the game. He tries to draw double coverage away from Freddie Solomon for the Walsh special.

To repeat, the crowd is on its feet as Joe Montana rolls right (almost to the sideline) and throws over Dallas defensive end Ed Jones to the back of the end zone, hopefully to Dwight Clark, who rises and makes "the catch." Now with a 1-point lead, Dallas responds with a 31-yard completion to Drew Pearson (his only catch) and a game-saving tackle by rookie Eric Wright. Lawrence Pillers of the 49ers not only sacks Danny White but forces a fumble, which is recovered by Jim Stuckey. For the first time in team history, the San Francisco 49ers are going to the Super Bowl.

11

1970 The last game before the merger brings the Minnesota Vikings and the Kansas City Chiefs to Tulane Stadium in New Orleans. Two suffocating defenses are the common denominator entering the game. The Vikings have allowed just 194 yards a game in total offense and the Chiefs just 226. Amazingly, both teams lead their respective leagues in pass defense efficiency with the same mark of 42.1.

Halfway through the 2nd quarter, the Chiefs are leading the Vikings 9–0 on 3 Jan Stenerud field goals, and they recover a fumble on the Minnesota 19. On 3rd and goal at the Minnesota 5-yard line the call is "65 toss power trap," and Mike Garrett scores for a 16–0 halftime lead. Dave Osborn caps off a 69-yard drive with a 4-yard run to get the Vikings on the board with 4:32 left in the 3rd quarter.

At this point in the game, quarterback Len Dawson of the Chiefs is 10 of 15 passing for just 103 yards in "matriculating the ball down the field." Now on 1st and 10 at the Minnesota 46-yard line, Dawson fires short to flanker Otis Taylor. Taylor breaks left corner Earsell Mackbee's futile attempt to bring him down. Leading 23–7 entering the 4th quarter, the Chiefs defense repels the next 3 Viking drives with interceptions. The Super Chiefs are champions.

1987 The Denver Broncos have beaten the Cleveland Browns seven straight times (8 of 11 all-time). In this more important first-ever meeting in the play-offs, the Browns have regained the lead late in the 4th quarter, 20–13. Coach Marty Schottenheimer's defense led the AFC in total defense during the season by allowing just 266 yards a game. The "Dawg Pound" is rocking, and John Elway has 98 yards to navigate to become a legend.

Mixing his plays masterfully, Elway runs and passes his team to the Cleveland 14-yard line. He scrambles 9 yards to the 5-yard line with 42 seconds left. Mark Jackson cuts hard inside and catches Elway's rocket for 5 yards and the tying touchdown. Rich Karlis's 33-yard overtime field goal wins the game for a Denver team that gains 374 yards in total offense in this matchup.

12

1969   The Baltimore Colts have scored 460 points and defensively allowed only 17 offensive touchdowns in their 16 games going into the Super Bowl. For the AFL Champion Jets to win, they must control the ball and stop the Colts. Four times the Jets intercept in their own territory to stop Colt drives. Fullback Matt Snell gains 71 yards rushing (121 for the game) on 16 carries in the 1st half and scores the Jets only touchdown of the game.

We are late in the 3rd quarter, and so far Joe Namath has completed 15 of 26 for 156 yards. Since the Colts have chosen to "roll coverage strong," Jets split end George Sauer has become Namath's main target, and on Namath's last 2 pass attempts of the game he delivers again with receptions of 11 and a game-long 39 yards. The drive leads to the final Jet score on Jim Turner's 9-yard field goal. The Colts' rally under John Unitas results in just 1 touchdown; thus the unthinkable occurs: New York 16, Baltimore 7.

1975 The "Chief," Art Rooney, has brought his Steelers to the Crescent City. Minnesota stands in the way on the Tulane Stadium turf. On their first 6 possessions, the Vikings record just one 1st down against the "Steel Curtain." Though Franco Harris gains 61 yards rushing on twelve 1st-half rushing attempts, the Steelers lead just 2–0.

A Pittsburgh fumble recovery on the kickoff leads to a 4-play 30-yard drive to take a 9–0 lead. Harris is a constant force in the 2nd half, as he carries the ball 22 times for 97 yards; thus he sets records for attempts (34) and yards rushing (158) in the game.

Now, late in the 3rd quarter, the "Steel Curtain" again pressures Fran Tarkenton on a 2nd and 12 play from the Pittsburgh 47. His pass is again deflected, and this time Charles Edward "Mean Joe" Greene intercepts. Early in the 4th quarter, after an interference penalty has given the Vikings 1st and goal to go on the Pittsburgh 1-yard line, the "Steel Curtain" forces a fumble, which is recovered by—you guessed it—Greene. A punt block touchdown by the Vikings closes the gap, but Pittsburgh responds with an 11-play 66-yard drive to score and put the game out of reach, 16–6. Rooney has his trophy.

13

1974 The defending Super Bowl champion Miami Dolphins are attempting to join the Packers as the second team to win back-to-back Super Bowls. We are in Rice Stadium in Houston, Texas, to witness a brutally precise offense (Miami) against the "Purple Gang" of Minnesota.

The Dolphins run 20 plays for 118 yards on their first 2 possessions and lead 14–0. Future Hall of Fame fullback Larry Csonka carries the ball 8 times on traps, counters, and dive plays for 64 yards. Future Hall of Fame quarterback Bob Griese completes all 4 of his pass attempts on the drives for 40 yards. Griese attempts just 3 more passes the entire game.

Early in the 3rd quarter, the Vikings and Fran Tarkenton face 3rd and 8 on their own 13, behind in the game 17–0. Defensive tackle Manny Fernandez sacks Tarkenton for a 6-yard loss. Miami begins their next drive in Viking territory, and 8 plays later, Csonka again powers his way into the end zone. Now with a commanding 24–0 lead, the Dolphin defense under coordinator Bill Arnsparger mixes fronts and coverages superbly in dictating the strategy of the game to Tarkenton and the Vikings.

Minnesota eventually scores, but the dominant Dolphins achieve history. Csonka gains a record-setting 145 yards on a record-setting 33 carries and heads to "Hole in the Wall" with his MVP trophy.

1991 A record crowd of 77,025 are in the Meadowlands to view Mike Ditka's Chicago Bears and Bill Parcells's New York Giants. The winner of this game earns the right to attempt to dethrone the two-time champion 49ers. The Bears' Neal Anderson gained 1,078 yards rushing in the regular season but today gains only 19 yards on 12 attempts against New York's 3–4 defense. The Giant's ground game, led by Ottis Anderson, gains 194 yards on 48 carries.

Quarterback Jeff Hostetler completes 10 of 17 passes for 112 yards, as New York amasses 23 1st downs. Chicago does not record a rushing 1st down for the first time in Bear play-off history. At 38:22, the Giants control time of possession and score in every quarter in the 31–3 victory. On to San Francisco and the NFC Championship.

14

1968 For the first time, the AFL–NFL championship will be played in the Orange Bowl in Miami. For the last time, Coach Vince Lombardi will be on the Packer sideline leading his men to victory. The Oakland Raiders' impressive victory over the Houston Oilers (40–7) gave rise to the belief they could beat a veteran Packer team.

Game MVP Bart Starr completes 6 of his first 10 passes for 113 yards. Leading 6–0 on 2 Don Chandler field goals, Starr, on 1st and 10 at his own 38, lofts a pass down the middle of the field to Boyd Dowler for 62 yards and a touchdown.

Daryle Lamonica needs to pass to rally the Raiders, who trail 26–7 in the 4th quarter. The Raiders begin the drive at their own 16-yard line, and now it is 3rd and 8 at their own 48. Lamonica's out-pattern pass to flanker Fred Biletnikoff is intercepted at the Packer 40-yard line by future Hall of Fame corner Herb Adderley. For the first time in Super Bowl history, a player returns an interception for a touchdown. All-decade guard Jerry Kramer asks his teammates at halftime to "win one for the old man." They win 33–14, and Vince Lombardi goes out a winner in his final game.

1990 For 40 years, the Rams and 49ers have battled for Western Division supremacy; this game will determine who represents the NFC in the Super Bowl. The Rams have won eight of their past nine games (their only loss is to the 49ers). The last two victories were road play-off victories in which the Ram running game produced 290 yards on 60 attempts (4.8). Earlier in the season, the Rams beat the 49ers in San Francisco, 13–12. Can they do it again?

Joe Montana completes 26 of 30 passes for 262 yards as he carves the Ram defense. While San Francisco pans for gold on the ground with 179 yards on 44 attempts, the Rams are stopped cold, as they gain only 26 yards on 10 attempts.

The Ronnie Lott–led defense intercepts 3 passes, as Ram quarterback Jim Everett completes only 16 of 36 in the game. The 30–3 victory gives the 49ers a ticket for a return trip to the Super Bowl. Can they win back-to-back Super Bowls for the first time in their storied history?

15

1967   The Kansas City Chiefs and Green Bay Packers are at the Coliseum in Los Angeles for supremacy—the right to be the first champion of a game played by the two rival leagues. For perspective, let us return to 1954 and two of the most intriguing men who play key roles in this game. Vince Lombardi is in his first year as an NFL assistant coach with the New York Giants. He goes on to lead an improved Giant offense to a winning season. Five successful years in New York and seven in Green Bay have brought him to the summit.

Max McGee is a rookie split end who caught 9 touchdown passes (the most of his career) for the Packers in 1954. McGee is no longer a key component in the Green Bay machine, yet Bart Starr relies on him over and over again on this day. We are at 3rd and 3 at the Chief 37, and Starr hits McGee on a post pattern (a one-handed catch) for the 1st touchdown in Super Bowl history.

Now we are in the middle of the 3rd quarter, and Green Bay leads 21–10. Can the Pack put away the Chiefs? Starr looks over the Kansas City defense on 2nd and 12 at his own 42, and fires to McGee for 11. Later in the drive, at 3rd and 11 at the Kansas City 44, Starr again throws to McGee and completes for 16 yards. The Packers pound away with future Hall of Famer Jimmy Taylor, and it is now 1st and 10 at the Chief 13.

Starr, for the first time, throws to McGee on 1st down, and McGee makes a juggling catch for his 2nd touchdown of the game. Starr to McGee accounts for 40 of the 56 yards gained on the drive. Leading 28–10 in the 4th quarter and on 1st and 10 from the Packer 45, Starr again goes deep down the middle to McGee, and again Max delivers. The 37-yard gain puts the ball on the Kansas City 18. The Packers go on to find the end zone again, for a final score of 35–10.

The Packer defense plays their usual brand of stifling defense, and Bart Starr earns his MVP award with his accurate passing and play calling. For so many though, the day belongs to a veteran receiver who caught 7 passes for 138 yards. McGee retains the record for yards receiving, until Lynn Swann's performance in Super Bowl X.

16

1972 Under Coach Don Shula, the Dolphins have won 20 of the 28 regular-season games they have played. Defeating the Chiefs and Colts in the play-offs has brought them to Tulane Stadium in New Orleans to take on the Cowboys. For five consecutive seasons Dallas has lost in the play-offs, yet now a new question arises after a road loss to the Bears. How tough are the Dallas Cowboys?

A seven-game win streak to close the regular season in which the Cowboy defense has allowed just 613 yards rushing (69 a game) has helped answer the question. Dallas opponents have scored just 7 touchdowns in the win streak (2 rushing and 5 passing).

Roger Staubach leads a revitalized Dallas offense into the Super Bowl. Coach Tom Landry calls counterplays in the 1st half in hopes that Nick Buoniconti and the Dolphin defense will overpursue. Dallas rushes for 124 yards on the ground in the 1st half.

Leading 3–0 in the 2nd quarter with 6:15 to play, the Cowboys begin their drive from their own 24. On 2nd and 9 from the Dallas 47, Staubach finds future Hall of Famer Lance Alworth open over the middle for 21 yards. Calvin Hill enters the game and gains 25 yards rushing to put the Cowboys on the Miami 7-yard line, 1st and goal to go. Game MVP Staubach fires into the left corner to where Alworth's precisely run pattern has taken him, touchdown Dallas.

Duane Thomas continues his fine running, and the Cowboys gain 128 yards rushing in the 2nd half to set a Super Bowl record of 252 yards rushing. Especially effective were sweeps to either side of the Dolphin defense.

It is the beginning of the 4th quarter, and future Hall of Famer Bob Griese is trying to rally the Dolphins from a 17–3 deficit. On 3rd and 4 from the Miami 49, Pro Bowl left linebacker Chuck Howley attempts to "chop block" Dolphin wide receiver Howard Twilley. As Howley scrambles to his feet, Griese's flat pass comes right at him. Howley returns the interception 41 yards to the Miami 9-yard line.

Staubach throws to future Hall of Famer Mike Ditka on a crossing pattern in the end zone, and the Super Bowl trophy finally goes to the Dallas Cowboys, 24–3.

17

1999 Setting a new regular-season scoring record with 556 points, the Minnesota Vikings are hosting the Atlanta Falcons in the NFC Championship Game. The Vikings finished fifth in the NFC in total defense, yet the emphasis in Minnesota is on their prolific offense. Wide receivers Randy Moss and Chris Carter have gained more than 2,300 yards and scored 29 touchdowns.

The Atlanta Falcons finished the regular season with nine consecutive wins. Running back Jamal Anderson averaged 120 yards rushing a game in Atlanta's 14 regular-season wins. He gained 113 rushing in the victory over the 49ers in the divisional round of the play-offs. Today, however, he pounds away for just 67 yards on 23 carries. Quarterback Chris Chandler picks up the slack by completing 27 of 43 for 340 yards. Tony Martin, with 5 catches for 129 yards, is Chandler's main target.

Minnesota has the ball and a 20–7 lead with 1:17 left in the 1st half. Defensive end Chuck Smith of the Falcons strips the ball from Randall Cunningham as he attempts to pass. Travis Hall recovers for Atlanta at the Minnesota 14. Chandler fires to Terence Mathis for 14 yards and a touchdown. Morten Andersen of Atlanta kicks a 27-yard field goal in the 3rd quarter to bring the Falcons to within 3. The Vikings respond with a Cunningham touchdown pass to Matthew Hatchette early in the 4th quarter.

Chandler hits Martin for 70 yards to set up another Andersen field goal. Now with only 2:07 left to play, Gary Anderson of the Vikings lines up to attempt a 38-yard field goal to put the game out of reach. He has made 46 consecutive field goals, but the streak ends (wide left). Now, with just 49 seconds left, Mathis finds an open area in the Viking end zone, and Chandler, avoiding the rush by rolling left, spirals the ball to him for 16 yards and the tying touchdown.

Atlanta starts from their own 9-yard line in overtime and drives deep into Minnesota territory. Now, the other Andersen again lines up and splits the uprights from 38 yards, and for the first time in their history the Falcons are going to the Super Bowl.

18

1976 For the first time in league history, teams that had already won a Super Bowl would face off. The Dallas Cowboys led the NFC in rushing (174 yards a game), and their young defensive line had improved with each week. The Cowboys outscored the Vikings and Rams 54–21 in the first two rounds of the play-offs.

The Super Bowl defending champion Steelers had allowed just 14 offensive touchdowns in their last 12 regular-season games (they won 11). Pittsburgh had allowed both the Colts and Raiders 1 offensive touchdown in their two play-off victories. The winner of this game continues on to join Green Bay and Miami as two-time winners of the Super Bowl.

With 8:04 left in the 1st half, the Cowboys take possession at their own 48-yard line with a 10–7 lead. Running back Robert Newhouse runs to the left on a 1st and 10 play at the Pittsburgh 20 and loses 3 yards as outside linebacker Andy Russell brings him down. Defensive ends L. C. Greenwood and Dwight White sack Roger Staubach on the next 2 plays. Now out of field goal range, the Cowboys punt. The Cowboys continue on to go 9 consecutive possessions without scoring. Welcome to the "Steel Curtain."

The Dallas "Doomsday" defense would be just as resilient, as the Steelers gain 178 yards in total offense on 63 plays, with the exception of 4 plays. Those 4 plays are Terry Bradshaw to Lynn Swann passes. Swann catches passes for 32, 53, and 12 yards (1 in each quarter) early in the game. At 3rd and 4 on their own 36-yard line with about 10 minutes left in the game, Dallas blitzes Bradshaw, yet he has time to unload deep down the middle to Swann, who scores on the 64-yard pass play to put the Steelers ahead, 21–10.

Though Staubach continues to attack the Steelers (82 yards passing on the next drive and a touchdown), the Steelers continue to sack him (a record 7 times in the game). When "Knotty Pine" Glen Edwards intercepts Staubach's last pass in the Steeler end zone, the game belongs to the black and gold, 21–17.

19

2003 The Tampa Bay Buccaneers have led the entire league in total defense by allowing just 4,044 yards (252 a game). Tampa Bay is on the road in Philadelphia for the right to go to the Super Bowl. Can their defense take them there?

Duce Staley's 20-yard touchdown run puts the Eagles ahead early. Buccaneer quarterback Brad Johnson's 71-yard completion to Joe Jurevicius sets up the tying touchdown. Johnson is a productive 20 of 33 passing for 259 yards in the game. From this point onward, the Buccaneers defense stymies the Eagles time and time again. Tampa Bay led the league in pass defense efficiency with a mark of 48.4

(the best in the league since the Vikings in 1988), and Donovan McNabb gains only 243 yards on 49 passes for the game.

Early in the 4th quarter, corner Ronde Barber intercepts and returns the ball 92 yards for a touchdown to put the Buccaneers ahead, 27–10. Tampa Bay wins for the first time in seven tries on the road in the play-offs (the Buccaneers also win for the first time in three NFC title game efforts). Coach Jon Gruden is headed to San Diego to face his former team, the Oakland Raiders.

The Raiders are at home in the AFC title game against the Tennessee Titans. The Oakland offense, led by quarterback Rich Gannon (the league MVP), averages 390 yards a game (the best in the league). Gannon gains 41 of his team's 89 rushing yards in the game and is his usual efficient self, leading the Raider-controlled passing game. Gannon completes 29 of 41 for 286 yards passing without throwing an interception.

Two Titan fumbles recovered by the Raiders deep in their territory result in Oakland leading 24–17 at the half. Entering the 4th quarter with a 3-point lead, Gannon takes the Raiders down the field twice on touchdown scoring drives to win their first AFC title in 19 years. The Raiders are AFC champions, 41–27.

20

1980 The Rams beat the Steelers twice in regular-season games during seasons when Pittsburgh won the Super Bowl (1975 and 1978). Could the Rams beat the Steelers in their first Super Bowl appearance? For 3 quarters, the Rams kept coming back to take the lead (6 lead changes). Jon Stallworth had played an outstanding game against Dallas in last year's Super Bowl, but so far today he has only had 1 catch for 3 yards.

It is 3rd down and 8 yards to go on their own 27-yard line, and reigning Super Bowl MVP Terry Bradshaw fires deep on "60 slot hook and go." Stallworth makes the over-the-shoulder catch and scores to give the Steelers a lead they never relinquish. Later in the 4th quarter, on a drive deep into Pittsburgh territory, future Hall of Fame middle linebacker Jack Lambert intercepts Vince Ferragamo's pass. With less than five minutes left, Bradshaw again goes to Stallworth deep, and again the future Hall of Famer delivers. His 45-yard reception puts the ball on the Ram 22. Five plays later, the Steelers score again. The team of the decade has won their fourth Super Bowl.

1985 The 1984 San Francisco 49ers were the first team to ever win 15 regular-season games. The matchup at the quarterback position was considered the key to the game. Would Joe Montana be able to match record-setting passer Dan Marino of the Miami Dolphins pass for pass? San Francisco's defense is effective on 3rd down, as Miami converts just 4 of 12 opportunities. San Francisco gains 537 yards on offense on 76 plays.

Assistant Coach Bobb McKittrick's offensive line blocks the Dolphins all day. Game MVP Joe Montana does his usual superb job of spreading the ball around, yet one 49er is the key offensive component. Roger Craig gains 58 yards rushing on 15 carries and catches 7 passes for 77 yards. Craig becomes the first player in Super Bowl history to score 3 touchdowns in a game (2 rushing and 1 receiving) in the 38–16 49er victory.

21

1979 The first regular-season game in Cowboy history was against the Steelers. The first Cowboy victory in their history came against the Steelers. The Cowboys are defending Super Bowl champions and have won 42 of their last 57 regular-season games and their last 5 play-off games. Standing in their way is a team that has won two Super Bowl titles (including one against Dallas). The winner of this game becomes the first team to have won three Super Bowl titles.

The Dallas defense had destroyed many a running attack during the 1978 season, as they led the NFC in that department by allowing just 107 yards a game. The Cowboys also ranked very high (fourth in the league) in pass defense efficiency, with a mark of 53.7. The Steel Curtain allows just 21 touchdowns in the regular season. Where would the scoring come from in this game?

Future Hall of Fame running back Franco Harris is limited to just 46 yards rushing in his first 19 carries. Game MVP Terry Bradshaw is on target in the 1st half, as he completes 11 of 17 for 253 yards and 3 touchdowns.

There is just one minute left in the 1st quarter on a 3rd and 8 play on the Pittsburgh 39. Future Hall of Fame quarterback Roger Staubach beats the Steelers man coverage with a dart to Tony Hill at the left sideline. Hill's 39-yard touchdown is the 1st touchdown allowed by Pittsburgh in the 1st quarter all season.

The game is tied at 14 with less than two minutes left in the half. The Cowboys face a 1st and 10 at the Pittsburgh 32. Future Hall of Fame right corner Mel Blount intercepts Staubach, and the Steelers drive 56 yards in 5 plays to go ahead at the half, 21–14.

It is now early 4th quarter, and Pittsburgh has a 3rd and 9 situation on the Dallas 22. The Steeler staple goes into effect—trap left and Franco Harris explodes for 22 yards and a touchdown (his last carry of the game). The Steelers recover the Dallas fumble on the kickoff, and Bradshaw fires down the middle on his last pass. Lynn Swann reaches up, and Pittsburgh is ahead, 35–17.

Dallas will not go quietly into that goodnight, as Staubach drives the Cowboys twice down the field to score as he completes 10 of 13 for 113 yards and 2 touchdowns. Rocky Bleier recovers the onside kick to ensure Steeler victory. The 35 points allowed by Dallas is the most since October 1973 (92 games).

22

1984 Acquiring veteran talent had long been a strength of Al Davis. When the Raiders put the final piece in their defensive puzzle in future Hall of Fame right corner Mike Haynes, they were complete. The Washington Redskins scored an impressive 541 points in the regular season (including beating the Raiders in a shoot-out). The Redskins are a confident group, having won 16 of 18 going into the Super Bowl.

Recovering a blocked punt for a touchdown and returning an interception for a touchdown (just before the half) help give the Raiders a 21–3 halftime lead. John Riggins found the silver and black 3–4 defense difficult to run against at the outset, as he gains just 37 yards on 16 carries in the 1st half. His Raider counterpart, future Hall of Famer Marcus Allen, is able to gain 44 yards on 11 carries. Allen proves to be the difference maker in the 2nd half, as he gains 147 yards rushing on just 9 carries. His 1st and 10

74-yard touchdown run on the last play of the 3rd quarter puts the game out of reach.

Mike Haynes's man-to-man coverage is brilliant (he intercepts Joe Theismann in the 4th quarter), and the Los Angeles Raiders are champions, 38–9.

1989 The Bengals are returning to the Super Bowl after a seven-year absence to again face the San Francisco 49ers. The resilient Cincinnati defense coached by Dick LeBeau gives ground but not points, as the Bengals lead 13–6 entering the 4th quarter.

Wide receiver Jerry Rice sets the Super Bowl record for yards receiving with 215 (including 5 catches for 142 yards in the fateful 4th quarter). Joe Montana's precision passing on the 11–play, 92-yard drive to win the game still ranks as the longest scoring drive to win a Super Bowl. Montana completes 8 of 9 for 97 yards on the drive. We bid a fond farewell to future Hall of Fame coach Bill Walsh. San Francisco joins the Raiders and Steelers as the only teams to win at least three Super Bowl championships.

23

2000 The only winning coach in Tampa Bay history, Tony Dungy, brings his Buccaneers to St. Louis for the NFC Championship Game. Entering the 1999 season, the Rams had won only 37 of their past 122 regular-season games. Coach Dick Vermeil's rebuilding plan has reached fruition as the Rams offense averages 400 yards a game.

It is the immovable versus the irresistible, as the Bucs allow an NFC-low 235 points and the Rams score a league-high 526 points. With less than five minutes left in the game, the immovable Buccaneers lead, 6–5.

The Ram defense, which allows only 203 yards in total offense for the game, gives their offense possession in Tampa Bay territory after a Dré Bly interception. Ram record-setting quarterback Kurt Warner finds veteran wide receiver Ricky Proehl on a 30-yard fade route up the left sideline for the winning touchdown.

Tampa Bay responds by driving to the Ram 22-yard line with a little more than a minute left. The key defensive play in holding off the Buccaneers is Ram defensive end Grant Wistrom sacking Shaun King. Although they score a season-low 11 points, the Rams are returning to the Super Bowl for the first time in 20 years.

2005   The AFC Championship Game brings the defending Super Bowl champion New England Patriots to Pittsburgh to play one of the two teams that beat them in the regular season (34–20). The Steelers enter the game on a 15-game win streak.

Pittsburgh outgains the Patriots 163 to 126 rushing and 225 to 196 passing, yet loses the game 41–27. New England leads 17–3 late in the 2nd quarter, but the Steelers are driving. Steeler quarterback Ben Roethlisberger underthrows an out pattern, and Patriot safety Rodney Harrison purloins the pass for an 87-yard touchdown.

Coach Bill Belichick's mistake-free Patriots continue to parlay Pittsburgh turnovers into points in the 41–27 victory. Tom Brady completes 4 passes to wide receiver Deion Branch for 116 yards and 2 touchdowns and a return trip to the Super Bowl.

24

1982   In his second season in Cincinnati, Coach Forrest Gregg guided the Bengals to the best record in the AFC.

The Bengals balanced offense was led by all-pro quarterback Ken Anderson. Cincinnati scored the third most points in the league with 421. They returned to the playoffs for the first time since 1975, when Anderson led the league in passing and his position coach was Bill Walsh. Now, six years later, Anderson again had the best passer rating in the league (98.4).

In the 12 regular-season Bengal victories, they averaged 138 yards a game rushing but only 78 in their four losses. Anderson had veteran deep threat Isaac Curtis and rookie Pro Bowl receiver Chris Collinsworth (who gained more than 1,000 yards receiving). Both Cincinnati and San Francisco had 6–10 records in 1980, but that fact didn't matter as Jim Breech approached the ball for the opening kickoff.

Isaac Curtis breaks over the middle to catch Anderson's pass for 8 yards on the first play from scrimmage (Cincinnati recovers a 49er fumble at the San Francisco 26 to start the game). Pete Anderson pounds for 2 yards and the 1st down. Anderson completes an 11-yard pass to tight end Dan Ross for another 1st down. Goal to go for Cincinnati! For the rest of the game, the Bengals go on to face an uphill battle.

Free safety for the 49ers Dwight Hicks intercepts Anderson's 3rd down pass. Turnovers hurt Cincinnati in a December loss to San Francisco, and again today they are the difference maker as the 49ers score 20 points due to Bengal mistakes.

There is less than a minute left in the half, and the 49ers lead 17–0 thanks to 3 long scoring drives of 68, 92, and 61 yards. Joe Montana completes 12 of 17 for 132 yards on those drives. When Milt McColl recovers a fumbled Bengal kickoff return, Ray Wersching gives the 49ers a 20–0 halftime lead on his 26-yard field goal.

Ken Anderson completes 13 of 15 for 143 yards on his 3 scoring drives in the 2nd half. This is not enough to overcome Cincinnati turnovers and the resilient goal line stand late in the 3rd quarter by the 49ers. San Francisco gains 275 total yards offensively, yet scores 26 points. Cincinnati gains 356 total yards and scores 21 points.

25

1981 Although they lost a hard-fought 10–7 regular-season game to the Eagles, the Raiders are relishing the rematch. Right outside linebacker Rod Martin drops to his zone on a 1st and 10 play on Philadelphia's opening drive. Martin returns Ron Jaworski's first pass 17 yards to the Eagle 30-yard line. Seven plays later, Jim Plunkett completes to Cliff Branch for the first Oakland touchdown.

The Raiders lead 21–3 in the 3rd quarter, and Martin again intercepts a Jaworski pass intended for tight end John Spagnola to halt an Eagle drive in Oakland territory. The game has all but been decided as the Raiders lead 27–10 late in the 4th quarter. Rod Martin becomes the first man in Super Bowl history to intercept 3 passes in a game, when he again "picks" Jaworski. Jim Plunkett provides the offensive fireworks as he gains 261 yards passing on 13 completions to earn game MVP honors.

1987 Bill Parcells brings his Giants to the Rose Bowl to face the Denver Broncos before a crowd of more than 100,000. The Broncos lead 10–9 at halftime, as John Elway has completed 13 of 20 for 187 yards against the nasty New York defense. His counterpart, Phil Simms, has completed 12 of 15 for 103 yards. When a quarterback completes 80 percent of his passes, he is considered on target, but wait . . . in the 2nd half Simms completes all 10 of his passes for 165 yards and 2 touchdowns. This record-setting performance still stands as Phil earns the game MVP in the 39–20 Giant victory.

1998 The defending Super Bowl champion Green Bay Packers are traveling west to San Diego to take on the wild card AFC champion Denver Broncos and their 37-year-old quarterback, John Elway. The Broncos led the AFC in both total offense and total defense, while leading the entire NFL in scoring with 472 points.

Running back Terrell Davis follows the exceptional blocking of his mobile offensive line for 157 yards and a record-setting 3 rushing touchdowns in a 31–24 victory. For the first time in 14 years an AFC team, and for just the second time a wild card team, has won the Super Bowl, as "this one's for John."

26

1986 In their first appearance in the Super Bowl, the Chicago Bears bring a defense that can dominate a game. The Bears have recorded 119 sacks in their 25 regular-season victories over the past two years. Can the New England Patriot offensive line give the quarterbacks time to throw?

The bruising Bear defense, coached by Buddy Ryan, led the league in fewest yards allowed rushing (82 a game) and pass defense efficiency (51.2). Bear opponents have scored just 22 offensive touchdowns in 18 games, including the play-offs.

The Patriots gain 7 yards rushing (the fewest ever in a Super Bowl) on 11 attempts and turn the ball over 6 times. Led by Super Bowl MVP Richard Dent and future Hall of

Fame defensive lineman Dan Hampton, the Bears record 7 sacks. Jim McMahon completes 12 passes for 260 yards as the Bears total 408 yards in total offense in the 46–10 victory.

1997   Coach Mike Holmgren has molded his Packer offense into a force to be reckoned with, as they lead the league in scoring with 456 points. Coach Bill Parcells has brought pride back to the Patriots, and they led their conference in scoring with 418 points.

Brett Favre completes 14 passes for 246 yards, yet, upon closer inspection, it is his long passes to Andre Rison for 54 yards and Anthony Freeman for 81 yards (both touchdowns) that put the Pack ahead 27–14 at halftime.

Parcell's Patriots rally as Curtis Martin runs 18 yards for a touchdown to close the gap to 27–21 in the 3rd quarter. Desmond Howard takes the ensuing kickoff and, on a well-blocked middle return, goes 99 yards for the game-breaking touchdown (the longest in Super Bowl history). Game MVP Howard sets a Super Bowl record for combined kick return yards with 154 on kickoffs and 90 on punts.

Future Hall of Fame defensive lineman Reggie White sets a Super Bowl record with 3 sacks (including back-to-back sacks in the 4th quarter), and his teammates contribute 4 interceptions in the 35–21 victory.

27

1991   Coach Marv Levy's Buffalo Bills are headed to Tampa to play the New York Giants. Jim Kelly's league-leading passing efficiency (101.2) is a main cog in the Bills offensive wheel, along with running back Thurman

Thomas. Buffalo led the league in scoring with 428 points. Bill Parcells and Bill Belichick have built the league's most difficult defense to score on, and they allowed only 21 offensive touchdowns. Buffalo was able to beat the Giants just a month earlier, 17–13. Can they do it again?

The Giants have set a 16-game season record of fewest turnovers in a season with just 14. When the two teams played in December, there was not a turnover in the game by either team.

There is 3:49 left in the 1st half, and the Giants are trailing 12–3 when new starting quarterback Jeff Hostetler begins a 10-play 87-yard drive for a touchdown. The Giants are right back at it to begin the 2nd half, as they drive 75 yards on 14 plays. Their time of possession is more than nine minutes. Game MVP Ottis Anderson scores from the 1 to give the Giants the lead, 17–12. Anderson has the key run on the drive with a 24–yard run off left tackle on 3rd and 1 at the Giant 47-yard line.

Late in the 3rd quarter, Coach Parcells chooses to go for the 1st down on 4th and 2 at the Buffalo 35. Right defensive end Bruce Smith tackles Anderson for a 2-yard loss, and the Bills have new life. Thurman Thomas, who gains 135 yards rushing on just 15 carries, explodes on a 1st down running play up the middle for 31 yards and the go-ahead touchdown, 19–17.

The Giants begin the 4th quarter with another long drive of 74 yards on 14 plays. It leads to a Bahr 21-yard field goal to get the lead back, 20–19. Time is of the essence, and with 2:16 left, here comes the Bills down the field on a 61-yard drive to set up Scott Norwood's winning field attempt, which is wide right, and the Giants win their second Super Bowl in five years.

28

1990   Coach George Seifert has inherited a very talented defending Super Bowl champion in the San Francisco 49ers. Dan Reeves brings his Broncos back to the Super Bowl for the third time in four seasons. The Broncos allowed only 23 offensive touchdowns in the regular season. Denver faces a 49er offense that led the NFL in scoring with 442 points and total offense with 6,268 (392 yards a game).

Future Hall of Fame quarterback Joe Montana is his usual precision self in the 1st half, as he completes 15 of 21 for 189 yards and 3 touchdowns. Jerry Rice catches 5 passes for 108 yards (Rice now has 323 yards receiving in his last 6 Super Bowl quarters).

San Francisco leads 27–3 at the half. Can Denver rally? Montana completes his first 3 passes for 71 yards in the 2nd half (2 for touchdowns). He sets the record for most touchdown passes in a Super Bowl game with 5. Jerry Rice sets the record for most touchdown receptions in a Super Bowl with 3.

There is no Bronco rally, as San Francisco scores the most points in a Super Bowl with 55 and the largest margin of victory (55–10). Game MVP Joe Montana has now thrown 122 passes in four Super Bowls and has never been intercepted.

1996   Can the Dallas Cowboys ever beat the Pittsburgh Steelers in a Super Bowl? The first ever Super Bowl played in Arizona provides the answer. Dallas led the NFC in rushing during the season with 137 yards a game. Pittsburgh led the AFC in run defense, allowing only 82 yards a game. Can the Cowboys move the ball against the stalwart Steeler 3–4 defense?

The Troy Aikman–led Cowboys gain 193 yards in total offense and lead 13–7 at the half. On 3rd down and 9 at their own 48 in the 3rd quarter, Steeler quarterback Neil O'Donnell overthrows Ernie Mills up the right sideline. Left corner Larry Brown intercepts and returns 44 yards to the Pittsburgh 18-yard line. Emmitt Smith caps a short drive with his 1st touchdown.

Pittsburgh outgains Dallas in the 2nd half 201 to 61 and rallies for 10 unanswered points. O'Donnell faces 2nd and 10 on his own 32-yard line with 4:15 remaining in the game. Again game MVP Larry Brown intercepts, and his 33-yard return puts the Cowboys inside the 10. Smith scores his 2nd touchdown, final 27–17.

29

1994   The San Diego Chargers, with their AFC title game victory in Three Rivers Stadium in Pittsburgh, have earned their first Super Bowl berth. They are set to take on the San Francisco 49ers at Joe Robbie Stadium in Miami, Florida.

The Chargers led the AFC in run defense by allowing just 87 yards a game. The Chargers secondary is a focal point of this game, since they face a prodigious passing game. San Francisco won 48 of their last 64 regular-season games yet had not played in a Super Bowl. Steve Young, for the fourth year in a row, led the league in passing efficiency and now set the single season record with a mark of 112.8. Upon closer inspection of Steve Young's 1994 season, if you do not stop him and his receivers, you are going to lose. Young completed 277 of 391 for 3,488 yards with 33 touchdowns and just 6 interceptions in San Francisco's 13 regular-season victories.

On the 49ers 3rd play after the kickoff, Young throws

down the middle to Jerry Rice for 44 yards and a touchdown. On the 49ers next possession, Young completes a 51-yard touchdown pass to running back Ricky Watters.

The Chargers drive 78 yards on 13 plays to cut the lead to 7 on Natrone Means's touchdown run. The rest of the half is all San Francisco, as they score on 2 more touchdown drives.

Young throws another touchdown pass to Jerry Rice in the 3rd quarter. San Francisco's 7th and final touchdown is the record-setting 6th touchdown pass by Young, a 7-yard completion to Jerry Rice (his 3rd touchdown of the game). Young completes 24 of 36 for 325 yards without throwing an interception in his record-setting performance. The 49er defense limits the Charger running game to just 67 yards and records 3 interceptions. San Francisco becomes the first team in league history to win a fifth Super Bowl title.

30

1983 Crank up that diesel. Hopefully though, before any cranking, you feed the hogs. There have been many teams and many nicknames, but the 1982 Washington Redskins must rank near the top in that category. They will be best remembered, however, for their ability to grind an opponent into the ground.

Don Shula's Dolphins went undefeated in 1972, capped with an impressive Super Bowl victory. Shula's Dolphins now face another Redskin team in his quest to earn a third Super Bowl ring. Although Coach Richie Petitbon's complex Redskin defense limits Miami to just 176 yards in total offense during the game, Washington does not take control of the game until the 4th quarter.

During the regular season, fullback John Riggins gained 553 yards rushing—a valuable contributor but not the main focus of Coach Joe Gibbs's offense. Gibbs and offensive line coach Joe Bugel decided to run Riggins behind their physical offensive line; thus the "hogs," with counter treys, straight dive plays, and off-tackle powers, lead Riggins on a sojourn to destiny. Riggins gained 444 yards rushing on 98 attempts in the three play-off victories over Detroit, Minnesota, and Dallas. "Riggo" went on to set Super Bowl records for yards gained with 166 and attempts with 38 in the game.

At 4th and 1 at the Miami 43, Gibbs calls 70 chip, an off-tackle power play. Not only do the hogs make their blocks, but Clint Didier also stalemates Dolphin safety Glenn Blackwood to eliminate force penetration. Tight end Donny Warren's reach block allows Riggins to turn the corner. Riggins breaks right corner Don McNeal's vain attempt to tackle him, and the diesel is cranked and running for the go-ahead touchdown.

Washington begins their next drive at the Miami 41-yard line. Riggins gains 22 yards on this final Redskin touchdown scoring drive, Washington 27, Miami 17. For the first time since 1942, a Washington team ends their season with a victory in the play-offs. Hail to the Redskins.

31

1988 The Washington Redskins and Denver Broncos had faced each other only four times in the 18 years since the merger, and here they are in the Super Bowl. The Broncos led the AFC in total defense (202 yards a game) and pass defense efficiency (62.9). They face a Redskin offense that averaged 371 yards a game in their 11 regular-season victories. Washington has had numerous lineup changes on offense, yet there is no doubt coach Joe Gibbs will have his team prepared.

Doug Williams has passed the ball with efficiency during the season but has appeared in only five regular-season games. Running back Timmy Smith has played in seven regular-season games. The constant in the Redskin offense is their offensive line ("The Hogs").

Down by 10 points entering the 2nd quarter, the Redskins respond with a record-setting performance. Washington scores 35 points on 5 successive drives. Those drives are worth noting for the yards gained per play, with 357 yards on just 18 plays. Washington leads 35–10 at the half.

Timmy Smith gains 204 yards rushing to set a record, and game MVP Doug Williams averages 18.9 yards a completion to power the offense to a record-setting 602 yards in total offense, final score Washington 42, Denver 10.

1993 The two-time AFC champion Buffalo Bills are meeting the Dallas Cowboys (the youngest team in the NFL) in the Rose Bowl. Tied at 7 late in the 1st quarter, Charles Haley forces Jim Kelly to fumble. Dallas lineman Jimmie Jones returns the deflected ball 2 yards for the go-ahead touchdown. The flame has been lit. Look out, Bills!

Dallas turns 9 Buffalo turnovers into 35 points. The Cowboys future Hall of Fame trio all have impressive performances offensively. Quarterback Troy Aikman gains 273 yards on his 30 passes, with 4 being touchdowns. Michael Irvin catches 8 passes for 114 yards and 2 touchdowns. Emmitt Smith gains 108 yards rushing on 22 carries. The Cowboys put points on the board in every quarter on their way to their highest-scoring Super Bowl ever, final score Dallas 52, Buffalo 17.